SPEAKING WITH
the SPIRITS of
the OLD
SOUTHWEST

Conversations With
MINERS, OUTLAWS
& PIONEERS
Who Still Roam
Ghost Towns

Dan Baldwin, Rhonda Hull
& Dwight Hull

Praise for Speaking with the
Spirits of the Old Southwest

"The number three has deep meaning in society, mathematics, religion, and, closest to my heart, paranormal investigating. Three is considered the number of harmony, wisdom, and understanding. The triumvirate of Dan, Rhonda, and Dwight embody the exceptional characteristics this number implies. Beginning with a delve into history, then following the clues, assembling them, and finally arriving at a conclusion, our trinity of investigators combine their unique skills and perspectives to bring you an intriguing and illuminating glimpse of the Copper State."

—Brian Cano, *The Haunted Collector*

"This book has a very special meaning to me because Arizona has a very special place in my life. It has a powerful energy and history that I believe goes right back to our origins on this planet. It is the finest place in my view to conduct psychic and historical investigations, and the use of a pendulum is one of the most accurate ways to divine the answers. There are so many fantastic stories to research especially in and around the state as this team has demonstrated. I am sure the readers will find this to be addictive reading."

—Christopher Robinson, *The Psychic Dreamer*

"Travel along with the adventuresome trio of Dan, Dwight, and Rhonda as they explore some of southern Arizona's most haunted locations. Although the threesome has their own special techniques for communicating with spirits of the beyond, they all share the same quest for learning new methods of assisting those who have crossed over. Learn the history and live the mystery!"

"*Speaking with the Spirits of the Old Southwest* is an intriguing journey through the history of long forgotten gold rush towns of Arizona. Rhonda, Dwight, and Dan, in their capacity as intuitives and pendulum experts, are able to bridge the gap between the living and the dead to give readers an emotional glimpse into the paranormal world that is all around us. Unlike other paranormal investigative teams, their focus is to help the dead…whether it be helping them cross over or just listening to what they have to say. A must read for both fans of history and fans of the paranormal!"

"If you are truly interested in investigations into the psychic world, this really is the right book for you. Especially their take of the old west cowboys, gun fighters, and outlaws who dominated their world in Tombstone. I have to say that the three people involved in this book are the top investigators in the world today. They are guided with such energy in finding the truth. The skills they share between them and their strong characters are an inspiration. This book leaves you wanting more, with a real longing to visit Arizona and Tombstone. I loved the cases and stories."

SPEAKING WITH the SPIRITS of the OLD SOUTHWEST

About the Authors

Dan Baldwin is the author, co-author, or ghostwriter of more than 60 published books. His paranormal works include *The Practical Pendulum, They Are Not Yet Lost,* and *Find Me— As Told to Dan Baldwin,* which are available in e-book and paperback formats. He is also the author of numerous award-winning novels including Westerns, mysteries, thrillers, and short story collections.

Amazon Page:

https://www.amazon.com/Dan-Baldwin/e/B0080Z24CO

Smashwords Page:

https://www.smashwords.com/books/view/666742

www.fourknightspress.com

www.danbaldwin.biz

Internationally known-Psychic Medium **Rhonda Hull** experienced the paranormal since early childhood. Her gifts include clairvoyance, clairsentience, clairaudience, clear knowing or claircognizance, psychometry, remote viewing, and mediumship. As a Psychic, she is able to provide insight and direction for her clients, which she believes leads to a stronger self -empowerment. As a Medium, Rhonda has the ability to connect her clients with loved ones who have crossed over. Some of her clients are producers, Hollywood executives, musicians, and celebrities.

beelieveparanormal@gmail.com

World-renowned Paranormal Researcher/Pet Psychic and Animal Communicator **Dwight Hull** has been investigating the paranormal for more than 30 years. He has been involved in thousands of investigations and has actively investigated Tombstone (Arizona), Alcatraz Prison, Terminal Tower, Sherwood Forest, Tower of London, the Bacardi factory, the Queen Mary, Mansfield Prison, and many more. His background in the military and as a police officer lends to his expertise in the paranormal field.

beelieveparanormal@gmail.com

SPEAKING WITH the SPIRITS of the OLD SOUTHWEST

Conversations With
MINERS, OUTLAWS & PIONEERS
Who Still Roam Ghost Towns

Dan Baldwin, Rhonda Hull, Dwight Hull

Llewellyn Worldwide
Woodbury, Minnesota

FIRST EDITION
First Printing, 2018

Book design by Bob Gaul
Cover design by Ellen Lawson
Editing by Patti Frazee
Interior photos courtesy of the authors except Bird Cage on page 90, Courtland, AZ, on page 16, Fairbank Hotel, AZ, on page 102 and Hoptown, on page 246 provided by Library of Congress

Llewellyn Publications is a registered trademark of Llewellyn Worldwide Ltd.

Library of Congress Cataloging-in-Publication Data (Pending)
ISBN: 978-0-7387-5674-5

Llewellyn Worldwide Ltd. does not participate in, endorse, or have any authority or responsibility concerning private business transactions between our authors and the public.

All mail addressed to the author is forwarded, but the publisher cannot, unless specifically instructed by the author, give out an address or phone number.

Any internet references contained in this work are current at publication time, but the publisher cannot guarantee that a specific location will continue to be maintained. Please refer to the publisher's website for links to authors' websites and other sources.

Llewellyn Publications
A Division of Llewellyn Worldwide Ltd.
2143 Wooddale Drive
Woodbury, MN 55125-2989
www.llewellyn.com

Printed in the United States of America

Contents

Foreword

"Not only is the universe stranger than we imagine,
it is stranger than we can imagine."
—Sir Arthur Eddington, *English astronomer*
(1882–1944)

You've likely heard or read about instances where an angelic presence appeared before a distressed person and provided relief or guidance. The source or identity of the angel can be debated, but the real, positive effect upon the person cannot. English astronomer Sir Arthur Eddington noted that "not only is the universe stranger than we imagine, it is stranger than we can imagine." It is in this universe that good people may appear as angels. To the dead.

In this book, psychic investigators Dan Baldwin, Dwight Hull, and Rhonda Hull discover that history is alive in many of the Arizona ghost towns. By working as a team, the trio brings distinct talents as a checks-and-balances approach to paranormal investigations. Dan is an accomplished dowser (pendulum) and author, Dwight is a paranormal researcher and animal communicator, and Rhonda is a sensitive with an array of gifts including mediumship and clairvoyance. Their collective track record is impressive.

Their approach to "ghosts," or spirits, active in certain locations, is one of courtesy and common sense—treat them as people without a body, as you would treat anyone else. Many of the following investigations peak when those confused or distressed are assisted by the team to "cross over" into the light on their horizon. Reassurance and assistance can go a long way. If you could be of assistance to someone, wouldn't you? Maybe that makes you an angel.

Readers appreciating investigations into the paranormal will enjoy the check and recheck process they develop—such as Rhonda sensing a presence, Dwight having an impression of a male, and Dan, facing away from them, posing the question "Is there a female here?" The pendulum swings "no." "Is there a male here?" The pendulum swings affirmative. Often Rhonda will ask a question of the entity and Dan's pendulum will swing—"Is there something keeping you here?" The pendulum swings "no," in keeping with Rhonda's intuition. And so on.

And, of course, there are the ever popular EVPs—electronic voice phenomena. Invited to speak, many of the characters leave audible messages on one or both digital recorders. Not heard on site, but in playback.

It is these quips that confound many, and give pause to consider that, indeed, history is alive, and often not what we thought.

—George Sewell

Introduction

Although this book is written in first person, there are three authors: Dan Baldwin, Dwight Hull, and Rhonda Hull. Dan has used his pendulum dowsing skills to help locate missing persons and to solve crimes for more than a decade and a half, but he was new to paranormal investigations of haunted places. Dwight and Rhonda have decades of experience researching and communicating with the spirit world.

The three shared a fascination with and a respect for history. The events related in this book allowed them to combine psychic skills with the curiosity to discover what really happened in the old days. After all, what better way to discover the past than to discuss it with the people who were there?

The team was guided by three overriding goals: to conduct historical research, to connect with the spirit world, and to assist spirits when needed and when possible. That last goal was key. They did not pursue this calling merely to build a collection of EVPs (electronic voice phenomena) like someone would collect stamps, coins, or comic books. To borrow a phrase, "when the spirit is willing" and when it was possible to help that spirit, they attempted to provide whatever service possible. Sometimes the system worked and sometimes it didn't. No one is perfect 100 percent of the time. Sometimes their service brought about a profound sadness and sometimes it brought about astounding and incredibly rewarding results. Both ends of that spectrum are written up in this book.

Dan Baldwin and Rhonda and Dwight Hull.

Dwight and Rhonda Hull: Investigating History Through the Voices of Those Who Lived It

Dwight and Rhonda Hull earned an enviable record in paranormal research, but did not like the term "ghost hunters" to describe the efforts recorded in this book. They never "hunted" ghosts, because spirits are around us all the time. They exist beyond a shadow of a doubt. And even if the spirits are not in a mood to communicate, they're still present. The Hull approach was to interact with spirits. The goal was to meet them, understand them, learn from them, and if necessary and possible, to help them.

What better source of historical research can there be than the people who lived the history being investigated? We believed paranormal research a valid approach to historical research. Apparently that is so. Research into books, records, and museums sometimes provides validation for the results of paranormal research. For example, after a long trek through mesquite brush to the ruins of the Clanton Ranch, the Hulls recorded an interesting EVP. A male voice said "a really bad 'brush sting.'" Later, they looked up the unfamiliar term and learned that it meant getting scratched up by desert scrub.

Rhonda said, "It's an interesting concept when you listen back to your EVPs and you hear terms you're not familiar with. You have to look them up just to understand a term from 150 years ago that hasn't been used in 150 years, and to us that's absolute real gold for what we do."

Contrary to popular belief, paranormal investigators don't have to wait until dark to make contact. Spirits are out at all hours of the day. "In 32 years of investigation I've gotten more results and more interaction during the day than I ever got at night. The witching hour is a bit of a myth," Dwight said.

So-called hauntings fall into two categories: intelligent and residual. Intelligent haunts are those in which the researchers and the subjects of their research interact. These encounters can be friendly, matter-of fact, or emotionally charged. Intelligent haunts were more prevalent in the research for this book.

Residual haunts play out like a sound recording on a loop. The spirits are unaware of the investigators and are reliving the past as it was. "Very rarely do we come across a residual haunting and when we do it's usually in the form of music or background noise," Dwight said. "Most often, I'd say 80 percent of the time, we're dealing with intelligent, interactive spirits."

Intelligent beings deserve intelligent treatment. Rhonda said, "They're just people without a body. You should treat them just like a living person."

Fear of ghosts and haunted places is unnecessary, as Dwight said. "I probably need to make this point very clear—people on a lot of these new ghost hunter shows claim they've gotten scratched and say, 'Oh, it's demonic. It hurt me. It's attacking me.' If that's all a ghost can do to you, my cat is more dangerous than any ghost out there. That's not an attack. There's never ever been a documented case of a person being seriously harmed by a ghost. Never. So, there is no logical reason for anyone to be afraid of them. Absolutely no reason at all."

During paranormal research, investigators are frequently startled. It can be surprising to hear a voice from seemingly nowhere, a popping or knocking sound from where nothing is moving, footsteps upstairs when no one is upstairs, and to experience other similar sights and sounds. That doesn't meant those experiences should be frightening. Too many people equate being startled with fear. They fear what they can't see. So, if they hear a noise and they can't see the cause they get scared. It's their own emotions playing on them. It's a sound. That's all it is. Dan said, "If the noise was created by a spirit, great! Don't panic. Stop. Breathe. And try to figure out the meaning—the message—in that sound."

That approach proved valuable during one of their investigations when a couple of mysterious knocks led to a "get out" type warning. See the chapter titled "Knocked Out."

There are places they entered with caution because they knew the energy was different and possibly hostile. Being careful is not being afraid. Their approach was just like the way they'd approach a living, breathing person. "I've never been any place I considered to be scary," Dwight said. "I've been in places I knew were hostile. I've been in places that were sad. But never where I felt intimidated or scared—but cautious would be a better word."

Just as we do and just as they did during their life on this plane, ghosts come and go. They travel if they want to—most of them. Encounters with trapped spirits are rare and sometimes, as the reader will soon discover, they can be heartbreaking.

Dwight and Rhonda have discovered that ghosts have the ability to travel pretty much any place they want to go. Some ghosts travel from place to place, from past to present, and even from this side of "the curtain" to the other side and back.

Rhonda said, "It's like a frequent flyer thing I guess. When you get over there. I've dealt with spirits at one location—through EVPs I know their voices—and I'll go to a different location and that spirit either followed me or is already at that location. It's the same voice, so that's an indication to me that they can move and go wherever they want."

The Hulls have even invited spirits to visit their home to just hang out. "They're just people without a body and they're welcome. We have our rules," Rhonda said. "There's no banging anything after we go to bed. Don't mess with the electronics while we're sleeping. That sort of thing."

Spirits can manifest themselves through all five senses. For example, during an investigation Dwight experienced the unmistakable taste of blueberry pie. The sensation came on quickly and unexpectedly. The host of the investigation later revealed that his deceased mom used to make him blueberry pie. Spirits seem to know what sense will trigger a response in the investigator, home owner, or person being contacted. Perfume and cigarette smoke are common smells used by or at least associated with spirit activity.

Everyone knows that houses can be haunted. Not everyone realizes that objects can also be haunted. Inanimate objects can hold the energy of a person who has passed. The grandfather clock in the Hull residence is an example. After they purchased the clock and brought it home the spirit of an old man showed up. The clock was broken, so they had someone come out and fix it. Once the repairs were completed and the clock was working the ghost disappeared from the scene and hasn't returned. They believe the spirit just wanted his clock fixed. Once that was done, there was no reason for him to hang around.

Paranormal research is a legitimate tool for learning history, but it is a technique that continually opens new and amazing areas of investigation. Dwight said. "When I began this work some 32 years ago I had a couple of questions. Today I'm up to about question number 502."

Dwight and Rhonda advise beginning and novice paranormal researchers to keep things simple. They discourage someone automatically buying the high-tech $500 cameras, the night-vision cameras, and this or that kind of a pod. A basic, good quality hand-held voice recorder and a camera are all anyone really needs. They also recommend getting advice from credible people with a good track record in the field—people who have written books on the field who have been doing it long enough to have real experience in a variety of paranormal situations.

Dan's advice is similar. There are many pendulum guidebooks available, including his *The Practical Pendulum*. Get one and study it. Buy a pendulum that looks right or feels right and practice for at least six months. Learn the movements, how to interpret them, and how to understand the subtleties that will be uniquely yours.

Rhonda said, "Do your research. And don't go into somebody's home and right off tell them they have demons because they may have some psychological issues. You don't make that assessment and then scare the crap out of someone. Get the evidence first. If you think there's something going on have them call in a priest. Don't make claims you can't back up."

The Hulls never provoked spirits. That's always been a cardinal rule. Spirits should be treated with courtesy and respect.

"I always treat spirits with respect," Dwight said, "even those who don't treat me with respect. You get more flies with honey than you do with vinegar. It's just like if you walked into a party and started yelling, 'Talk to me! I demand that you speak with me right now.' People are going to look at you like you're stupid. And you are. But, if you go in and say, 'Excuse me, I appreciate you having me here. Can we maybe sit and talk a little bit?' That's what's going to get you the results. It's the same with spirits. You go in and you treat them with respect and you'll build a relationship and won't be a ghost hunter chasing someone through a house. You'll be someone invited to have a conversation. You have to give them respect."

As with dealing with the living, hostility is inevitable. If someone is angry and hostile on this side of the curtain, chances are very good he or she is angry and hostile on the other side. It's a difficult thing because hostility takes different forms, and people perceive hostility differently. Opening up cabinets at night isn't necessarily a hostile act. It could just be a way of getting attention. Such activity could still frighten a homeowner, especially someone with little or no experience in or knowledge of the paranormal world. Instead of reacting with fear or anger, Dwight and Rhonda recommend acting pretty much as you would with a living person. Just ask the spirits to stop. "And I know it sounds like a very simple solution to what may appear to be an overwhelming problem, but it really does work," Rhonda said.

If an investigator meets hostility with respect more often it's going to take care of that supposed hostility. A lot of times supposed hostile ghosts are only trying to get attention. They've tried other things, but no one paid attention. The initial attempts to respond or make contact went unnoticed, so the spirits keep ramping up their game until someone pays attention.

A Psychic on Training Wheels

Although Dan has studied, learned, and taught pendulum dowsing and has used the technique to locate missing persons for more than a decade and a half, he often feels like a newcomer to the field and describes himself as a "psychic on training wheels."

He is quick to point out that a pendulum is nothing more than a weight on a string. The weight can be anything—a rock, metal, wood. It doesn't matter. The string can be actual string, a necklace chain, fishing line, or whatever. It is merely a means to an end. The important thing to remember is that the pendulum is just a tool. It's a hammer, a pen or pencil, a computer, and that's all. The rock on a string doesn't really do anything except act as an indicator of psychic activity. It is a way to work with the dowser's subconscious mind. When someone swings a pendulum that busy-body called the conscious mind becomes occupied with the movement, which frees the subconscious up to do its work. There's no magic in a weight on a string. The magic, if that's what you want to call it, happens when that tool enhances the connection between the dowser, his subconscious mind, and a higher power.

The dowser allows the weight to swing in a circle. A right swing usually means "yes" and a swing to the left generally means "no." A pendulum can only provide yes/no type answers. The dowser can't ask multiple choice questions because there can't be a yes/no answer. "Is the missing person to my north or to my south?" must be rephrased. "Is the missing person to the south?" "Is the missing person to the north?" A back-and-forth swing in any direction means the operator should ask the question in a different way.

Beginning dowsers should understand that the strength of a pendulum does not indicate a degree of right or wrong. A strong swing isn't more correct than a weak swing or vice versa. The difference is often just a reflection of the energy available at the moment.

It's a slow process, but an accurate one.

The biggest challenge for the dowser is to achieve and maintain a clear and objective mind so that the conscious mind doesn't shift into busy-body mode and take over. "It's like the old saying: Be careful what you want because you might get it," he said. "For example, if I'm looking for a missing child, I want that child to be alive. If I let that emotion allow the conscious mind to shove out the subconscious mind, I'll get the answer I want. 'Yes, she's alive and well.' The actual situation may be just the opposite of what I want. Worse than that, my efforts to find that missing person will be hampered or ruined by my allowing my emotions in."

Dan's process involves the following steps: (1) Pray in. (2) Meditate. (3) Set up psychic protection. (4) Set the intention for the session. (5) Ask: Can I do this? May I do this? Should I do this? (6) Conduct the session. (7) Monitor accuracy throughout the session. (8) End the session. This process is explained in detail in *The Practical Pendulum.*

Dowsing isn't limited by time and space. For example, dowsers can locate missing persons or objects hundreds, thousands, or tens of thousands of miles from their work stations. Dan never hesitates to state that nothing is 100 percent accurate. Dowsers are subject to the same conditions that affect everyone else. A dowser with a bad case of the flu is going to have a bad day swinging that rock on a string. A fight with a spouse, alcohol or drug use, a lack of concentration, superstitions, fatigue, outside distractions, or any number of factors can affect accuracy.

He said, "When dowsing, relax. Keep an open mind. Don't let emotions take charge. And remember that you're doing good and important work. Keep swinging."

A Combination of the Three

Dan and Rhonda met while working missing persons cases. The three got together and became close friends when they started exploring Arizona's ghost towns, ghost mines, and other ancient and historical sites. At some point the light bulb flashed on and one of them said, "Do you think we could combine intuitive skills with pendulum dowsing to conduct paranormal research?" The idea was so obvious that they decided to conduct an experiment to see. The results of that initial experiment are detailed in chapter 1.

Obviously, the concept worked, but it was and still is a matter of trial and error, profound sadness and incredible joy, and continuing efforts to fine tune the process. The combination of three distinct skills brings a new dynamic to paranormal research. The intuitive approach works. The pendulum dowsing approach works. But each has its limits. Combining skills overcomes many if not all of those limitations.

The intuitive approach is often not in real time. Even though certain of contact, the researcher must return to the home or lab to get confirmation—usually in the form of an EVP. Sometimes the response would be heartbreaking. Dwight said, "Before we could feel them, yes, we could get all that, maybe we could get an EVP after we got home. We'd hear a cry for help and it was, 'Oh, God, we have to go back.' But working with a dowser we're getting more real-time answers. With the right questions we're able to narrow the box down so that we can help the spirits right there and then instead of having to go back. The dynamic of having a dowser with us is to me a very welcome thing."

Rhonda said, "It's a missing piece. It's a great new feature to what we do. I think that now we have the whole package."

The team employed intuitive skills, dowsing, and the appropriate technical equipment to do a much more intensive and thorough investigation at the site. All the bases were covered. Only three people were involved, which tended to make the spirits less intimidated and more willing to communicate. Working as a team, they were able to short-circuit the normal process. One of the real benefits was the ability to ask follow-up questions immediately on site. The EVPs when captured were always valuable, but the investigators were no longer hampered by a need to discover, enhance, and understand those EVPs before continuing.

The validation of the psychic information was immediate. The first and the final chapters of this book prove just how important immediate validation can be.

These transcripts are presented here in the same conversational tone that occurred in real-time. The intention is to give you a sense of being there. A paragraph break is indicative of a pause, which most often happened in order to give the spirit time to respond.

The great lesson of this book is that people are people. Regardless of which side of the curtain they're on, people continue. Their emotions continue. And for many, there is a continuing need for understanding and help. That's really what this book is all about.

To listen to the EVPs go to:

www.beelieveparanormal.com/our-book.html

1

Jail Break in Courtland, Arizona

Our first paranormal work led to a jailbreak.

Our intuitive/pendulum experience at the Courtland Jail was a trial run and not originally intended as the basis for a chapter in this book. The visit was just an experiment. When we decided to conduct paranormal investigations— for lack of a better term, "ghost hunting"—in historical sites we did not know if our skills would mesh. Rhonda is an intuitive who can see, feel, and hear spirits. Dwight is also intuitive and has an investigative background through his military service. I have more than 15 years of experience in pendulum dowsing, as a volunteer to help find missing persons and solving crimes.

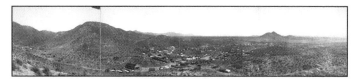

A panoramic view of Courtland, Arizona, from 1909.
Courtesy Library of Congress.

We wondered if our skills would mesh. Even if the skills worked well and in concert, we still didn't know if the three of us could work effectively as a team. We felt it was highly probable that psychically the sum of the parts would be greater than the usual result from individual action. But we didn't *know*. A great concern was that we might not get any results at all. Our individual skills were proven, but there was the possibility that they might cancel each other out.

The big challenge early on was to determine just how we would go about our research. The intuitive process is free flowing. Pendulum dowsing engages the psychic realm, but the process must follow certain basic and unalterable rules. The gift of intuition doesn't require such a strict process, mostly an open mind and heart. What process should we use to combine these related but very different skills? It was obvious that the different skills would serve as validation and backup for each other.

We decided that Rhonda would be the primary lead in asking questions, at least in the initial phases of any given investigation. Of the three of us she was the most skilled at recognizing and contacting those who had crossed over.

We decided early on that one of us could take over the role of questioner if that action felt right at the time. That chore often fell to Dwight, whose attitude of respect seemed to strike a chord with many of those who have chosen to make contact, or at least respond, to our efforts.

Would all of this work and would it yield positive results?

And that's what the trip to Courtland was all about. Initially, we considered it a trial run. As things turned out, the results of that experiment were far more interesting, successful, and dramatic than we at that time thought possible.

Boom 'n' Busted in Courtland

Courtland, Arizona was typical of the boom towns that were founded on dreams, built on greed and hope, and busted by the reality of played-out mines and dramatic shifts in the national and world economy. The site, now a ghost town, is at the southeastern tip of the Dragoon Mountains and only 14 miles from the one town that refused to bust—Tombstone. Courtland was named for Courtland Young, one of the owners of mining interests throughout the area. Established in 1909, the adobe, rock, and brick town held the promise of great and long-term wealth wrenched from the copper deposits below ground.

Courtland's population peaked at 2,000 and for a time it was quite a booming place. The town had numerous businesses, including restaurants, grocery stores, general stores, pool halls, hotels, land brokers, a bank, meat market, barbershop, and a railroad station. People could even call each other on the telephone to arrange a get together at the local baseball diamond or at the horse races. The town was typical of many in the early days of the West. Cosmopolitan saloons shared many of the same customers as the squalid brothels down the street. Upscale tycoons walked the same streets as low-life scoundrels and decent folks just trying to make a living. As long as the mines produced, money flowed and the streets stayed busy. Often, blood flowed in the same streets.

That was the boom. The bust began in 1917 when the copper started playing out. The mining companies began to show a loss of profit and then took a nosedive into the red on the ledger books. The town newspaper, *The Court- land Arizonan,* closed down in late 1920 and the exodus was quickly followed by the owners of the business community. The post office closed in 1942, and today the town, what's left of it, is a true ghost town.

Originally, the town jail was an abandoned mining tun- nel with a wooden door. When a prisoner set his mattress on fire to burn down that door, he nearly suffocated. The townsfolk found $1000 to build a true jail and constructed what soon became one of the most popular buildings in town. The structure was built of concrete reinforced with steel; much of that steel from railroad ties, rails, and other scrap metal. It had two 14' x 15' cells connected by a 6' x 8' center office. Each cell had a sink and a toilet. The Courtland jail became popular with law-abiding miners and other inhabitants because it offered so much more in terms of comfort than their shacks, cabins, and canvas tents. Over-crowding became a serious problem, not so much because of the amount of lawbreaking in town, but because of all the lawbreaking in town specifically designed to end up with a pleasant night under a sound roof.

The jail was called "Bright's Hotel," an homage to Deputy John Henry Bright.

Today, severely damaged, trashed, and covered in graffiti, it is the only remaining complete structure in Courtland.

A Different Vibe

Dwight and Rhonda came across the Courtland Jail by accident. Avid historians, the two intuitives invested a considerable amount of time exploring ghost towns, abandoned mines, haunted houses, and sites of historical interest. During one of these explorations they drove south on the appropriately named Ghost Town Road, which connects the ghost towns of Pearce, Courtland, and Gleeson in Cochise County, Arizona. Passing through Courtland they noticed the one remaining building and stopped for a look.

Dwight said, "We looked all around there and got some feelings about that area."

Rhonda added, "The jail had a different vibe. When we drove around that corner and saw that jail, the building just pulled to us. There was something about that jail that really called to us."

The authors each agree that listening to and following the directions of one's subconscious is essential, not only in paranormal research, but in living fully our daily lives. That nagging thought in the back of your head is information trying to get out.

The different vibe in Courtland is easily explained. A jail would naturally be a repository for all kinds of negative vibes: anger, depression, regret, fear, and so on. Those emotions would likely be magnified due to the large number of inhabitants who passed through. For example, a house may be haunted by one or even several spirits, but a jail could hold the energy of dozens of former (and possibly current) inmates. When they walked into the building, Dwight and Rhonda had the feeling that it held residual energy—spirit activity that repeats as if being played on a recorded loop. They also sensed intelligent activity in which the spirits are aware of and can interact with people in the present.

Dwight and Rhonda carried digital voice recorders on these journeys and they decided to conduct an electronic voice phenomena (EVP) session. No voices, mysterious sounds, or unexplained events were recorded during that trip. Despite that lack of success, Dwight commented, "There was always that lingering thing inside both of us that there was something there whether they talked to us or not.

There was that lingering pull to go back at a later date and check it out."

The Courtland Jail was selected for our trial run for two reasons. One, Dwight and Rhoda felt strongly that the place was inhabited by spirits. They felt the chances of making contact were good. Two, since the sessions and recording would be conducted inside a building, interference from outside noises—such as wind, animal sounds, or passing traffic—would have a minimum, if any, effect on the recordings. The goal was to capture Class-A EVP responses—clear, unmistakable voices making clearly understood statements.

The Time Was Right

Rhonda said, "Immediately I picked up on at least two spirits—two male spirits, like a father-and-son age bracket." She explained the term "older" as it applies to spirits. "That doesn't mean one is older in years, but in terms of being more advanced spiritually when he crossed over."

She sensed the spirits from the moment we arrived, but for some reason they did not show themselves to her. "But I could definitely feel them and hear them and I definitely knew there was male energy there," she said.

Dwight felt much the same. "I knew it was going to be different this time. I didn't know why at the time, but I definitely knew there was male energy in that space."

I didn't feel a damn thing. Not only was this area of the paranormal new to me, I am a pendulum dowser and I've never claimed to be an intuitive.

We were enthusiastic about what we were going to attempt, but we didn't know if our experiment would work or end up in failure or, like Courtland itself, go bust.

The reader should note that the events we experienced occurred in broad daylight. We didn't wait until midnight for "the spooks to come out." We didn't light candles, bring out a Ouija board or employ exotic instruments. We didn't conjure anything with mystical incantations or employ any ceremony. Basically, we just walked in and said, "Hello. We'd like to talk."

We explored the cells and selected one for our experiment. Right away we heard footsteps from the other cell. We were the only people physically in the jail and, in fact, in the entire town at that time. The footsteps sounded like someone walking in shoes; not like an animal slinking by on the outside of the building.

Rhonda immediately felt a presence, a presence that wanted to communicate. "I felt a sadness, not as powerful as we felt later during that session, but I felt that there was a need to talk," she said.

Rhonda's intuitive impressions run the gamut from the briefest flash of insight to communication with a full-figure apparition. Emotional feedback from the spirit was a common experience for her. "Sometimes it's like they really want you to feel what they feel."

Dwight picked up a sense of urgency. It was time to conduct the experiment. We used two digital recorders and a video camera with sound recorder during the session. It's curious, but sometimes when two recorders are employed in capturing EVPs, only one will make the capture. We didn't want to take any chances and from that session on we've always used at least two recording devices in every session.

The big question remained: Could we combine intuitive gifts with pendulum dowsing?

Doing Hard Time

During the readings I sometimes conducted my pendulum work with the pendulum visible to Dwight and Rhonda. Just to make sure that one side wasn't subconsciously reading the other, a number of sessions were conducted with me facing away from them. My pendulum was obscured so that they could not see and perhaps be influenced by the movement. There was no difference in the two different types of readings. We continued to employ this technique every once in a while as a reality check on our accuracy.

Dwight has a calm and inviting manner when dealing with the other side, and we decided that he should take the lead on this investigation. He opened the session with a friendly and respectful introduction and an explanation of what we were about to do. In most cases early on we used pendulum dowsing as backup—a way to verify what Rhonda and/or Dwight had picked up. Rhonda sensed immediately that things were happening. As the session went on I was "swinging my rock on a string" and backing up their feelings. Rhonda felt that one of the spirits was standing between us, whispering in her ear. She was certain that one of the spirits had a name beginning with the letter W. "We all felt it. It was a very sad energy," she said.

We determined that one spirit was more advanced (older) than the other and that his self-appointed task was to act as a caretaker for the less advanced (younger) spirit. The older spirit had crossed over, but had come back to this side as caretaker because the younger spirit feared what he believed would happen to him when he crossed over. Apparently he felt a sense of guilt so strong that he was convinced he'd be sent to hell for his sins. Rhonda said, "I think he was living in his own hell already."

Dwight said, "I think he was afraid of judgment. That's what was keeping him on this side."

During the session I was silently asking questions while using my pendulum to confirm what Dwight and Rhonda were getting. I'll be the first to admit that I am not a skilled intuitive, but I was definitely feeling a strong sense that this spirit was terrified of crossing over. The feeling was undeniable. I didn't believe I was picking up something from my fellow investigators; I felt this emotion was coming directly from the source.

We asked if there was anything we could do to help improve the situation.

Each of us felt a "yes."

Busting Out

Rhonda felt the emotions most intensely. She said, "He was still afraid. He was a little bit resistant. Seriously, I felt like I needed to give him a hug. He just needed to know that it was okay to cross over. He was just somebody afraid of dying because he was afraid of the judgment. I didn't really feel like he was a bad person in life, but he had a lot of guilt and shame."

"You don't have to be a bad person to feel like a bad person," I said.

Dwight said, "You could feel the energy ramping up. Rhonda started and I chimed in. We said, 'We give you permission that you can go ahead and cross over.' There is no judgment there. The individual who is with you is going to help guide you. You don't have to worry about anything. You're allowed to go. We're giving you permission to go and actually be at peace."

As Dwight spoke each of us independently was overwhelmed by emotion. It burst upon us without warning or build-up. It wasn't a matter of one of us affecting the other; the feeling came on much too fast for that. Rhonda was looking at the floor. Dwight was monitoring the scene on his video camera. I was looking directly down at the pendulum. I felt what I can only describe as a "sad release." It was, to me anyway, as if this spirit was happy to at last escape from jail, but had a realization that he could have left at any time.

I said, "He's gone."

Dwight said, "It was really an intense build up. There was a release and it felt clean. I don't know how else to explain it."

Rhonda said, "It was a big rush of clean energy."

Later when reviewing our recordings, our notes, and our feelings I told Dwight and Rhonda, "I knew intellectually what you guys do, but that was the first time I have experienced what you do. I thought, 'Whoa. I see what this is all about now.' We didn't just say, 'Hey, we've got an EVP; let's go home and listen to it.' We really helped somebody in serious need."

Dwight said, "It encompasses all your senses. This time you could actually feel it, physically feel that release. It was very tactile."

Rhonda said, "That's what makes such a big impact in what we do."

"It was a great day," Dwight said.

Dwight said of the Courtland experience, "For us it was different because we've never worked with a pendulum dowser before. When you do an EVP session you normally ask general questions and hope to get answers. With the pendulum you get immediate answers to your questions way out 'there,' but as you start getting specific answers to your questions you start fine tuning more and more. You start getting better answers because you're asking better questions. It was neat how we brought all our skills together."

"You can narrow it down very quickly with a pendulum as opposed to just having a recorder," Rhonda said. "We may hear something we can validate immediately whereas you can't with a recorder because you're recording. You have to go back and listen to the recording in a quiet environment. It's a different perspective and it's definitely more effective. Even though we're only able to ask yes/no questions, it narrows down the process so quickly."

The events of the day proved to us that the concept of combining our skills would work and would work very well. We began looking for new sites to explore that very day.

The EVPs

R: You need to let go and…

DB: I'm feeling a sense of relief.

R: Me too.

EVP: Thank You.

To listen to the EVPs go to:

www.beelieveparanormal.com/our-book.html

A Little Bit of Heaven in Kentucky Camp

Combining the skills of two intuitives with the skills of a pendulum dowser required time, experience, patience, a willingness to experiment, and a desire to face the unknown. The transcript of one of our earliest investigations shows how this process evolved and was tried, tested, and refined to our current approach. We traveled to an abandoned but well-preserved ranch site near Sonoita, Arizona, called Kentucky Camp, where we encountered an interesting relationship between two spirits and were faced with a serious question about the nature of our work and the ethical questions that work inevitably brings up.

*Dwight and Rhonda stand outside
of the bunkhouse at Kentucky Camp.*

*The interior of
Kentucky Camp's bunkhouse.*

*Dan is near some of the ruins
at Kentucky Camp.*

Arizona is known as "the Copper State," but it is gold that first attracted explorers, adventurers, miners, settlers, and the rough-and-tumble times that followed. One of the sources of that wealth is the Santa Rita Mountains located today in the Coronado National Forest.

The Santa Rita Water and Mining Co. built Kentucky Camp in 1904. The idea was to channel water through a pipeline seven miles from the mountains for use in hydraulic mining. A water cannon was used to blast away the rock and dirt so the miners could get to the gold within. The venture lasted only two years. Problems with the water supply, combined with the mysterious death of the chief engineer in 1905, caused a shut-down in 1906.

For the next 50 years the facility served as the head-quarters for a cattle ranch, but was later sold to a mining firm. The Coronado National Forest acquired the property in 1989 and it is now listed on the National Register of Historic Places. The ten-room headquarters house, where we conducted our research, is one of the largest surviving adobe structures of its era. Four other adobe buildings are also on the site. People who want to get a small taste of what ranch life was like can even rent a three-room adobe building for an overnight stay. One of the original hydraulic cannons is on display near the old gold processing building—the metal slowly rusting and joining the elements of the mountains it tried to destroy.

Kentucky Camp is located in a beautiful area surrounded by rolling hills and nearby mountains. We parked at the top of a hill and walked the old road down into the camp hoping for contact, but not quite expecting the results we got. We toured the site and enjoyed touching history before settling into comfortable chairs in the headquarters.

The interaction that occurred during this session reinforced the concept that spirits aren't just spooks waiting around to shout "boo!" at some unsuspecting visitor. They're people who experience the full run of human emotions. Sometimes, as in human relations on this side, those emotions can be in conflict. People who disagree in life can still disagree in life after death. The realm of the spirit world would prove to be much more complex than traditional thought would have us believe. The encounter at Kentucky Camp was just the first of many eye-opening experiences.

Dwight began the session. My references to "that's a yes" or "I'm getting a no" and so on are in response to pendulum movements.

D: EVP Session One. We are at Kentucky Camp. We are in what I guess is the headquarters building. It is April 9, 2016 at approximately 3:28 p.m. And currently we are in one of the small rooms off the main hallway.

DB: Are there any departed spirits here?

That's a pretty good yes.

D: Yep.

DB: Are you willing to communicate with us?

Kind of a weak yes.

R: Were you miners here at the camp?

DB: yes.

R: Did you find a lot of gold?

DB: Yes.

R: Did you die here? Did you pass at the camp?

DB: You need to ask that another way. "Are there more—"

R: Are there more than one of you?

DB: Yes.

R: Okay.

DB: You can't get a yes or no on a multiple choice question.

R: Right.

Are there about five of you here?

DB: Yes. A strong yes. You need to address one of them.

R: Did any of you pass at the camp? Die at the camp? Any of you?

DB: Yes.

R: Okay.

(**Commentary:** We are just beginning to learn to format questions in a way that enhances each set of skills. Use of a pendulum requires asking yes/no or either/or questions.)

D: I would like to ask if there are any people here with us. We are doing a pendulum session so you can manipulate that for yes or no answers. Also I would like to ask if you could call out your names. If any of you are here could you call out your names so we can record it? My name is Dwight. That is my wife, Rhonda. And that is our very good friend Dan. So you know who we are. We'd like to know who you are. So anytime during this session just come up to us and say your name very loudly and clearly and we can understand you on this little box here. It's called a recorder. That would be great.

Are there any females here?

(**Commentary:** Dwight's intuitive skills had already picked up something. He asked a question in such a way so as to prevent influencing Dan's use of the pendulum. Notice he didn't say "I sense a female." At this point we were learning how to fact-check each other's responses.)

DB: I'm getting a yes.

D: If there are females here I'd like to welcome you. Are there females here under the age of twenty?

DB: I'm getting a yes.

R: Did you live here with your parents? Did the females that were under twenty?

DB: That's a yes.

D: Okay, to the female here, I always like to know why you're here. Are you here just because you liked it here?

DB: Yes.

D: I can understand. It's a very quiet, very nice location.

DB: Are you here *now* because you like it here—in this timeframe?

That's a yes.

I can't say that I blame them. It's a wonderful place.

D: If you're going to be someplace this is the place to be.

R: Absolutely pretty.

D: For anybody here, males or females, was this building used for any purpose other than as a company building? For management? Let me phrase the question again. To your knowledge was this building ever used for anything other than management?

DB: Yes. Pretty good yes.

(**Commentary:** The references to "strong" or "good" or similar modifiers throughout this book refers to the strength of the pendulum swing.)

R: It looks like a lot of rooms. Did people sleep here? Like the miners?

DB: Yes. Yes. Yes.

R: Did you stay here?

DB: Is there more than—

R: Right. Did any of you stay here in this room when you were alive?

DB: Yes.

R: Okay.

D: Let me ask this question of anybody who is here— was this building ever used at one time as a hospital or infirmary?

DB: Yes.

D: I'm getting a strong sense now, and have been, that there were sick people here.

R: Right. It's more like a hospital.

DB: It makes sense. You'd obviously bring them here.

R: Right.

D: I'm seeing sick people?

R: TB?

D: Or something like that. I'm seeing non-mine related diseases. The female comes across to me that she was here. She was in this building and she was sick.

To the female who was here, to the female who was sick. Were you here because you weren't feeling well?

DB: That's a yes.

D: I imagine because of the type and size of the building it was used for many purposes.

DB: Probably a catchall building.

D: An everything building.

R: To the female who is here, did you pass due to a contagious disease?

DB: Yes.

R: Okay.

DB: Did you pass here, at this location?

Yes.

I'm curious. Is there anyone here now who is unhappy to be here now?

No.

D: Yep. That's exactly ... that's the first thing that came into my head—no.

DB: I'm not even getting a no.

R: You got a nothing.

DB: Null (movement). What are you guys getting?

R: Is there anybody here not happy in this place?

DB: That's a yes.

For some reason I asked the question wrong.

R: Is there anybody here who needs help in crossing over?

DB: That's a yes.

Was that person a female?

Again, yes

I was thinking no, but I got a yes. What are ya'll picking up?

D: I'm not picking up a stuck situation.

R: Maybe she's confused and not stuck.

Do you need help or are you trying to help someone else?

DB: One at a time. One question at a time. No two-part questions.

R: Sorry. To the female, do you need help? Okay, I'm going to rephrase that.

DB: It's swinging … It's swinging no.

R: Are you trying to help someone else who is here who is a female?

Okay. (Responding to a "yes" comment from the spirit.)

DB: That's a yes.

R: Is this person a man that you're trying to help?

DB: Yes.

(**Commentary:** Again, Rhonda's intuition led to questions that were validated by an independent source.)

R: Is the male stuck here?

DB: Yes.

Is the man who is stuck here happy anyway?

Yes. He's happy with it.

R: So maybe he doesn't need help, but she wants him to go. Is that—

DB: Swinging yes.

R: Has the male already been into the light and crossed over?

DB: Yes.

R: Yeah.

R: He just likes it here. He wants to stay here and you don't like it here and don't want to stay here.

DB: Say that again. Say it in—

R: Right. So, as I understand it, you would like him to leave this place.

DB: Yes. That's swinging yes right away.

R: [It's like she's saying] Enough already, we've been there/done that, let's do something else.

DB: Is he hesitant to move on?

That's a strong yes.

R: Then he's crossed over, but he just likes it here.

DB: Likes it here.

R: Okay.

D: Nothing we can do with that.

R: You're just going to have to work a little harder on that—work it out between you two. I didn't pick up anything that anybody had not crossed.

DB: That's why I asked if anybody was unhappy because I don't feel unhappiness here.

D: Oh, there's not … I don't feel unhappiness here.

R: It's just that she's not unhappy here but she wants him to go with her.

DB: And he's saying, "We've got a pretty good deal here."

D: I'm not picking up that it's her daddy. I'm not even picking up that it's a relation.

R: No. I don't think so.

D: I think it just might be somebody she knew.

DB: Is he a friend?

D: I'm picking up that he's older by quite a bit actually.

DB: Is the male we are discussing older than the female? Big yes.

Are you related by blood?

That's a no.

R: Well you can just get along if you want.

D: You can't make somebody go.

DB: Do we have the right to insist that someone move on? No, we don't.

D: No.

R: No.

D: If he's happy and he's where he wants to be …

DB: This falls into "none of our business."

R: That's between you and him.

If he hadn't crossed over that would be a different story.

DB: Is it true that he has crossed over, but has returned because he likes it here?

That's a strong yes.

D: Yes.

R: It's a beautiful place.

DB: Essentially our work is done. I don't think we should—

D: I don't think we should push the issue.

DB: That's not our job.

R: You're going to have to work it out between you guys. Once you cross over that's something you have to figure out—where you're going to be, what you're going to do.

DB: They're obviously not in a bad place.

R: If he's happy being here, so be it.

Shoot, I'd love to live here…

It's a little piece of Heaven.

Our goal in this area of paranormal work is to find and help spirits in whatever ways they may need help. We're not in the business of collecting EVPs and storing them in a computer file for later playback. In those cases in which we find a spirit content to remain where he or she is, we don't push the issue. The rights of privacy and personal choice extend beyond the grave.

3

Mattie Earp

One of the facts we discovered early on was that apparently the beliefs held on this side of life can be stronger than the reality available on the other side. These feelings often present themselves in the inability or even the fear of crossing over and continuing with the next level of experience. We faced a sad realization directly related to that, which presented a tough question: How do you help a spirit who refuses your help?

"When I began paranormal investigations I had five or so questions," Dwight said. "I've been at it more than three decades and now I have more like 500 questions." The list jumped to 501 questions after a visit with the spirit of Celia Ann Blaylock.

Dan uses a pendulum to communicate with the spirit of Mattie Earp.

Dwight and Rhonda in the Pinal Cemetery, where Mattie is buried.

Mattie Earp's tombstone in Pinal Cemetery.

Celia Ann Blaylock is an obscure Westerner better known as Mattie (Mrs. Wyatt) Earp. Her relationship with the man who, according to the television show theme, was "brave, courageous, and bold," lasted only 18 months or less and came to an abrupt and ultimately tragic end when Wyatt left Tombstone for good—without Mattie. Wyatt and Josephine Marcus lived as man and wife for decades and enjoyed adventures in Arizona, California, and even Alaska that have filled numerous books. Mattie faded into the backwaters of Arizona history and died a sad, lonely, and heartbroken woman.

Her relationship with Wyatt is documented in the 1889 U.S. Census: Earp, Wyatt S., age 32, brother, married, Farmer, born Ill. Earp, Mattie, age 22, wife, born Iowa.

Mattie may have arrived with Wyatt in 1879 or perhaps she arrived in Tombstone in 1880 and met him at that time and place. The records are as confused as the memories from which they were often taken. They may have had a formal marriage ceremony, but there is no record of it and it is generally accepted that she lived as his common law wife.

Apparently she suffered from headaches, possibly migraines, which may explain her addiction to the pain killer laudanum. She had other reasons to seek relief or escape in a bottle. While living with Mattie, Wyatt pursued and eventually won the heart of actress Josephine Marcus. Timothy W. Fattig in his *Wyatt Earp, the Biography* speculates that the women forced Wyatt into a decision between two very different lifestyles. As matters were judged in the Wild West, Mattie had a level of middle-class respectability, something Wyatt and his brothers craved. "Josey," sometimes called "Sadie," Marcus represented freedom, adventure, comfort in Western life, and a willingness to gamble for fame and fortune. Considering Wyatt's personality and history, his choice was inevitable.

When he left Tombstone for good in 1882, he left with Josephine on his mind and in his heart. They married and lived together for the next 47 years.

Mattie seems to have been a responsible and hard-working woman. In the 1930s, Virgil Earp's wife, Allie, offered her opinion of Mattie to writer Frank Waters. Allie said that Mattie was "as fine a woman as ever lived. She worked [hard] ... Stuck with him through thick and thin. And [she] was there every minute." If Mattie was bitter and heartbroken it seems that she had good cause.

The last recorded business between Wyatt and Mattie is a $365 mortgage on their Tombstone home on First Street signed on February 13, 1882. Mattie moved into the Cosmopolitan Hotel on February 20, 1882, and in March was again using her maiden name of Blaylock. She never left Arizona. She never saw or heard from Wyatt Earp again.

Mattie ended her days in Pinal, Arizona, a tough mining camp just south of the Superstition Mountains. Today Pinal is little more than rubble and trail ruts. The most prominent historical features can be found at the old cemetery across Highway 60.

Silver was discovered in the mid-1870s on Queen Creek far north of Tombstone, which led to the discovery of the hugely profitable Silver King Mine. An estimated $42 million worth of silver was extracted between 1875 and 1900. Milling was done in a new town called Picketpost, which became Pinal in 1878. Population estimates run from 800—2,000 during Pinal's glory days. The town was abandoned after the 1889 shutdown of the Silver King. Most of the people moved a few steps to the east to the small town of Hastings—today's Superior, Arizona, east of Phoenix-Mesa.

Only the faintest of ruins mark the small town where Mattie Earp died. Her life there is mostly a mystery. She had enough funds to rent her own apartment and when she died she left a number of pieces of fine jewelry.

Her body was discovered in that apartment on July 3, 1888. She was buried on Independence Day—a sad touch of irony you will understand when you read the results of our session. It is generally accepted that Mattie committed suicide by mixing laudanum and alcohol. The testimony of laborer T.J. Flannery in the coroner's inquest supports that view.

Q: What is the name of the deceased, if you know?

Flannery: Mattie Earp.

Q: Did you ever hear the deceased threaten her own life?

Flannery: I have. Earp, she said, had wrecked her life by deserting her and she didn't want to live.

Mattie was only forty years old. She was buried in the Pinal Cemetery. After Pinal folded, the cemetery fell into disuse. Today there are efforts to keep up the historic site and to show a bit more respect to the remarkable people who built this part of the state.

The people of Superior and the surrounding ranches and properties have a paternalistic attitude toward Mattie Earp's final resting place. At one time it was clearly marked with a column and even a photograph, but that has been torn down to discourage vandalism and desecration. A small, dignified marker has been placed within the cemetery in her honor. It does not mark her gravesite. However, for those willing to conduct in-depth research, the actual gravesite can be identified.

That location is where we conducted our paranormal session, where we met Celia Blaylock, a.k.a. Mattie Earp, and where we received a stunning surprise about her condition.

We often hear the question, "How do you know you're really speaking to the real spirit of a departed soul? Isn't it possible that a spirit is lying to you?" In most cases it is impossible to be 100 percent sure. A liar on this side of the curtain may continue to be a liar on the other side. Just as the living have many reasons to mislead, those on the other side may have motivations to mislead. That's why conducting as much research before beginning an investigation is so important. The more an investigator knows, the less likely he will fall victim to a lie. Additionally, in many cases the intense level of emotion that we have encountered to us eliminates the possibility of lying in many cases. That is certainly the case with Mattie Earp. There is no doubt in our minds, or our hearts, that we spoke directly with this poor lady's spirit.

D: Good morning, Mattie. Hopefully you're here with us this morning, hon. We came all this way to talk to you.

R: We came from Tombstone, which is probably not a great memory for you.

D: We know who you are. We only know the story that the history books have of you, which probably isn't the right story.

DB: Excuse me, I was neutral* until you said "probably not the right story" and it started swinging *yes.*

Are we speaking to Mattie?

I'm getting a yes.

D: Mattie, thank you for being here with us this morning. It's a beautiful morning. Mattie, let me ask you a question. It is said that your death was ruled a suicide. Is that true?

DB: I'm getting a *yes.* A weak response, but *yes.*

D: I'm going to guess it was unintentional. Is that correct?

DB: No.

D: Okay. It was intentional.

DB: Yes.

D: We're sure sorry to hear that, Mattie. In the scheme of things and what you were going through I think if I reach way far down I understand.

Mattie, are you happy now?

DB: No. I got a good response when you said that you understood.

R: Yeah. There was a big swing.

DB: The pendulum swung pretty wide on that.

D: We do understand.

R: Is there something we can do to help you where you're at?

DB: Yes.

(Dwight asks that Mattie speak into our recorders)

D: If there is something you can say that we can do to help you that would be great.

DB: I'm getting a *no.*

R: Are you with your family?

DB: No.

D: Do you know that you can be with your family now?

DB: Yes.

D: Is there something keeping you here?

DB: No.

R: Have you forgiven yourself?

DB: That's a *no.*

R: Have you seen your family since you crossed?

DB: No.

R: I think that might help. I really do. I think that might help your...

DB: Excuse me, she's saying *no.* That may be what she believes.

D: Mattie, are you embarrassed because of the way you died?

DB: Strong *yes.*

D: That's the feeling I got.

DB: That's a big *yes.*

D: Mattie, you don't have to be... I know this is easy for me to say, but... are you embarrassed about the way you died? There's no judgment. Your family's not going to judge you.

R: They'll be happy to see you. Really, they will.

DB: On the "judgment" I was getting a yes.

R: There is no judgment. I don't care what you were taught here when you were living.

DB: She's saying no.

R: Were you taught that if you commit suicide you go to hell—you're in your living hell?

DB: Immediate yes.

R: That's not correct. It's okay to go find your family. Nobody's going to judge you. It will make you so much happier. I just know that.

DB: I'm getting a no. She's got some strong beliefs.

D: She does have strong beliefs. Mattie, I'm not really sure what to do for you. You don't stay here and please don't …

R: Don't stay where you're at. You need to go find happiness. You need to let go of that belief that there's going to be judgment.

DB: Strong no.

R: Nobody can help you but yourself. Nobody can help you but you. You have to be the one to make that choice to let that go. God isn't going to judge you. It's nothing but love when you go over there.

DB: Neutral.

R: I'm sure your family will be happy to see you. What do you think?

DB: No.

R: There's not much we … I can't take your hand and guide you. All I can do is tell you that it's good.

DB: No. We're dealing with some powerful resistance here.

R: You know that the former Pope, the one before the current Pope, came out and told everybody that there is no heaven or hell. It's what's within you. Meaning there is no judgment when you die, when you cross. There is no judgment. That came from the Pope of the Catholic Church. So you can argue the fact and be resistant, but I'm just letting you know that you can go.

DB: Solid no.

D: Mattie, are you punishing yourself for doing what you did?

DB: Immediate yes.

D: That's what I thought. I'm sorry to hear that Mattie, because you don't need to. I know that's easy for me to say, but you really don't need to.

DB: She's saying yes.

D: Okay.

DB: That's just her belief.

D: I respect that. I don't understand it, but I respect it. And I respect you for your beliefs.

R: It's been about 130 years and I don't know how long you plan on punishing yourself, but that's quite long enough.

DB: I got a no. When you said "that's enough" I got a no.

D: You're in a beautiful scenic spot here. I'm sure you know that, so if you're going to spend more time here this is the place, I guess.

DB: Yes. And then a no.

D: That's a good answer. Yes and no. Okay, Mattie…

DB: She should know there's a way out if she wants to take it.

R: You know that, right? There is a way out if you want to take it.

DB: Nope.

D: You're a strong woman, Mattie.

DB: Yes.

D: You know what? I respect that. There's not much we can do for you. So I guess we'll close it down then and thank you.

R: Since you talked to us we'll come back and address whatever we need to address.

D: Thank you for your time. Thank you for allowing us to be with you. We're not that far away. Like we said, we're from Tombstone so we can come back. And we will come back if we need to. Absolutely. This is what we do.

DB: There was a *yes* on that.

D: Would you like us to come back some time?

DB: Immediate yes.

R: You're free to come to our house, too. Just letting you know. You can come visit.

D: Okay, Mattie, we're going to go. But we will be back…

DB: (Interrupting) She's gone.

D: (Continuing) Again, thank you for allowing us to be here.

DB: The pendulum just slipped out of my fingers.

D: I'll take that as a goodbye. A strong woman. She's a headstrong woman.

DB: I think we're telling her what she knows but what she doesn't believe.

D: Or doesn't want to believe.

DB: Thank you, Mattie.

Mattie Earp made the choice to remain in the Pinal Cemetery. You will notice in reading the transcript of the session we were not collecting EVPs like someone would collect stamps, coins, or arrowheads. Rather, these efforts are aimed at building a relationship with those who have crossed over, and in gaining a better understanding of their individual situations. That relationship may be momentary as in the cases in which the departed are helped to move on. The relationship may be long-term as in the cases in which spirits choose to remain. Maybe in time we or some other psychics will be able to help Mattie Earp forgive herself and move on to a better place.

In the meantime, she will not be forgotten or ignored. We are going back for more visits. Until another and perhaps better day, we will continue the relationship now established with Mattie Earp so that she and her life will not be forgotten.

*Reference to pendulum movement.

Sources for more information about Mattie Earp include:

Mattie: Wyatt Earp's Secret Second Wife by E. C. Meyers

Wyatt Earp: The Life Behind the Legend by Casey Tefertiller

The Earp Papers: In a Brother's Image by Don Chaput

When Silver Was King by Jack San Felice is an excellent source on Pinal and the Silver King Mine.

4

Ancient Voices at the Presidio

One of the questions that, excuse the phrase, haunt us is how spirits from other cultures and from so many different time periods are able to speak English.

For one thing, not all EVPs are in English. Other languages have been recorded in English-speaking countries. For example, Dwight and Rhonda once picked up an EVP recording of an unknown language. They were playing it for a friend in a restaurant in Tombstone when an Apache man approached. He said that the voices on the recorder were speaking Apache. He understood every word spoken.

Dan by the ruins at the Presidio.

Dwight and Rhonda by a marker at the Presidio.

Some of the ruins at the Presidio.

Dwight suggested a logical answer for those spirits who are able to interact with humans living on this plane: they listen and they learn. As modern people enter a place where spirits exist, the spirits hear English spoken. It's natural that with constant exposure throughout the years they'd pick up the language. One of the best ways to learn a language is through total immersion.

Consider a place like Tombstone's Birdcage Theater and the tens of thousands of English-speaking tourists who have been through there. Even a remote place such as the Presidio of Santa Cruz de Terrante has had a good bit of traffic since the 1700s. Ancient languages and Spanish, English, and a bit of other modern languages have been spoken there for hundreds of years.

We hiked to the ruins of the Presidio of Santa Cruz de Terrante in 2016. If successful, we expected to encounter cowboys or perhaps Apaches. If we were lucky we hoped to encounter one or more of the Spanish soldiers or support people who lived there several hundred years ago. Much to our surprise, one of the sessions we conducted put us in touch with and speaking with a culture from a time when speech was just beginning.

Presidio of Santa Cruz
de Terrante—Terror on the San Pedro

On August 22, 1775, an Irish mercenary named Hugh O'Connor chose a bluff overlooking the San Pedro River for one of three presidios (forts) he was constructing. The site is a still-remote place a few miles west of Tombstone, Arizona. The road to the trailhead leading to the presidio and the trail itself is easily accessible, although a bit of an easy walk is involved. Several adobe walls remain and the foundations of many others are visible. Structures include the remnants of a fortified wall and gate, a chapel, soldiers' barracks, commandant's quarters, guardhouse, and a bastion in which a cannon was placed.

A thick-walled square fortification worked well in many places and had proven its design value in Europe and the Middle East for thousands of years. It wasn't such an effective deterrent in Apacheria. The Apaches were extremely competent and aggressive guerilla warriors, possibly the best the world has ever seen. The unorganized tribes and clans fought off Spaniards, Mexicans, and Anglos for more than 400 years. In the early years of colonization the warriors used tactics and weapons that the Spaniards just couldn't overcome. The presidio lasted only five years. The last commandant wrote to the Spanish Crown in 1781, "The terror instilled in the troops and settlers of the presidio of Santa Cruz that had seen two captains and more than eighty men perish at the hands of the enemies in the open rolling ground at a short distance from the post, and the incessant attacks which they suffered from the numerous bands of Apache, who do not permit cultivation of the crops, who surprise the mule trains carrying effects and supplies, who rob the horse herds and put the troops in the situation of not being able to attend their own defense, making them useless for the defense of the province."

The soldiers, farmers, priests, and others did not have long to wait before hostile Apaches began to harass the settlement, attacking anyone who ventured out for water or tried to plant crops in the nearby fields. The Apaches were attracted by the large number of horses kept at the settlement and ran off the herds whenever they were unguarded. As the number of their horses became fewer, the soldiers were less and less able to pursue the raiders to reclaim their stolen mounts. It became a war of attrition and a very one-sided war it was.

Nearly a hundred men—just on the Spanish side of the battles—perished in less than five years. If there ever was a site for paranormal exploration, Santa Cruz de Terrante had to be included on our list.

When we headed out to visit the presidio we hoped to contact one or more of the troopers or someone supporting the troopers—Spaniards. Who we did encounter within those crumbling adobe walls was an astonishing surprise.

DB: We're going to be doing a session here. I'm working my pendulum and Rhonda's going to be asking questions. I've already gotten that there are spirits here. The spirits are willing to talk and be recorded. I hope I'm correct. I'm getting a yes.

R: Are there any women … how many women … oh, wait …

DB: You have to ask yes or no questions to narrow it down.

R: Okay, are there less than ten women here with us now?

DB: Yes.

R: Are there less than five women here with us now?

DB: No.

R: Okay, are there seven women here now?

DB: No.

R: Are there eight women here now?

DB: Ah, yes.

R: My mind just went blank.

DB: Welcome to the club. I especially admire the women who came out here.

D: Oh, tough, tough. Unbelievably tough.

DB: I'm getting a no.

R: Were you very frightened all the time?

D: Yes.

R: Did you have children?

DB: Did any of the women have children?

Yes.

R: Did the children work out here? For lack of a better word, did they work with their fathers?

DB: Yes.

Let me ask … is there one spirit here who would like to speak for everybody?

Nope. Everybody wants to chat.

(laughs) Yes.

R: Is Commander Tovar here?

DB: No.

R: Is there a commander here? Commandant?

DB: No.

D: I sense Indian here. I think that this is Indian.

R: Okay.

DB: Are we speaking to Native Americans?

Ah, yes.

R: Okay.

D: Is this your home that we're sitting in now?

DB: Yes.

D: I thought so.

It was a dome home, wasn't it? It had a round roof.

DB: That's a yes.

D: This is a big area. Was this a gathering area?

DB: No.

D: No. It was a home. Okay.

R: Did you have many children? Were there many children here?

DB: Yes.

R: I apologize for asking about the commandant.

DB: Were there white men in the area at the time you were here?

No.

D: No. This was before the fort.

DB: That explains those artifacts on the ground.

R: Yeah.

(The dusty ground revealed the occasional worked stone artifact outside the perimeter of the Presidio indicating a Native American presence prior to the arrival of the Spanish pottery shards from times prior to European invasion, for example.)

D: Before the fort this was a round building with a domed roof.

DB: Like a big wikiup.

D: Exactly like a big wikiup.

DB: Was this a communal home?

Yes.

I'm stopping the (pendulum) movement after every question, so we start fresh.

D: I can see it in my head. I'm almost to the wall of it here. And it was big.

DB: Big yes.

D: It was a big area and I'm seeing a round roof like a dome covered with animal skins.

DB: Yes.

DB: Did the men hunt with what we call a bow and arrow?

No. This may be really old.

D: Spears … did they hunt with spears?

DB: Yes.

R: Wow. I'm so glad they can communicate with us speaking English. Interesting.

Are you Ho Ho Kam?

DB: That's a yes.

D: This is pottery right here. It just showed up.

(Dwight noticed a pottery shard dating from the Ho Ho Kam era on the ground at that moment. These ancient Native Americans lived in Arizona 1700 years, arriving from Mexico in 300 B.C.)

Honest to God, it just showed up.

R: We want to preserve some of your history.

DB: Your stories are very important to the three of us.

R: Did you have a ball court in this area?

D: No.

R: Okay.

D: I am so in the moment now. I can see exactly—

R: Were there mastodons when you were here?

Elephants. Big creatures with tusks.

DB: I don't think they understand the question. I'm getting nothing.

R: Well, it wouldn't have been an elephant back then … big creature with a long trunk? And big horns. And it was *big*. Did you see those when you were here?

DB: Nothing.

R: Ah … Did you have big cats? Big tigers?

Is that a nothing or—

DB: It's a small yes.

They had jaguars here back in the day.

R: (speaks to Dwight) What's that?

D: A piece of bone. I believe a piece of bone. Again it kinda' just showed up.

DB: That's a yes.

R: Did you have big animals? Did you hunt big animals when you were here?

DB: Did the tribe hunt big animals?

Yes.

How tall was the wikiup?

D: You could stand in it.

Were the animals that the men hunted as tall as the structure you lived in?

That's a yes.

Were the animals the men hunted long haired? Shaggy?

Yes.

D: These were the Clovis People.

R: Did the animals that the men hunted have horns?

DB: Yes.

Did they have horns, what we would call tusks, as large as a man?

Yes.

DB: I think we're in ancient, ancient times.

D: They were Clovis.

DB: Yeah. Did the spear points the men hunted with have a groove down each side of the blade?

Clovis or Folsom. One or the other.

We're definitely in *pre*-historic times.

D: Yeah. We are literally right in the middle of a structure.

R: Did you learn English from the people who come out here in today's time?

DB: Yeah.

Is language ever a barrier of communication between your side and our side?

That's a yes.

But you understand us?

Strong yes.

D: Yes, strong yes.

Is there anything on this land close to us that we should know about?

DB: Yes.

R: Is it a sacred place?

DB: No.

Should we know about a burial place?

Yes.

Is the reason that we should know it is to honor the lives of those who have passed on?

Yeah. They want us to honor the deceased.

We're willing to do that.

R: Now we just need to know which direction it is. Is the burial place close to the river? Near the water?

DB: Every place out here is near the water.

R: Okay, is there a direction—

DB: No.

D: I don't think they want us to go there. I think they want us to—

R: To honor—

D: They want us to know—

DB: They want us to know that they were here.

D: That they were here. And not only are we honoring, of course, their dead, we're honoring them.

DB: Big swing yes.

That's a common human drive—we were here.

D: Right. They want us to know they were here.

DB: Big swing yes.

R: A lot of people know that the Spanish were here, and of course the Apache, but …

DB: I'm getting a no.

See, they don't know about the Spanish or Apache.

D: They were gone before them.

R: So after you were here there were other people here. But most people don't know that you were here. So, I guess that can be our story to tell—that you were here?

DB: Nice strong yes.

R: We can educate those who come out here.

DB: Is it important for us to tell people that you were here? Yes.

D: Yes.

DB: That your people were here first.

Strong yes. They're the forgotten people.

People know about the cowboys and the Apaches and the Spanish and the Mexicans, but—

D: Everybody talks about them, but nobody—

R: Talks about them.

DB: They're the forgotten people.

You want us to tell other people about you ... that you were here?

Yes. They're okay with it.

D: We will tell your story. We will tell people that you were here. And in doing so hopefully will honor you and the dead on this land.

DB: Strong, strong yes.

D: Very interesting.

DB: Yes.

R: Are you happy over there?

DB: Yes.

R: It's a good place. Am I right?

DB: Yes.

D: We are happy that you have taken time to communicate with us. We're happy that you have allowed us to come here and share your space and in return we will do everything we can to tell your story and to tell people that you were here first.

DB: A nice strong yes on that.

An interesting question came from this interview. Notice that at one time the spirits said they were Ho Ho Kam culture, yet clearly from the descriptions we got we were speaking with people from the Clovis Culture who inhabited this part of Arizona 10,000 years earlier. We didn't know and still don't know if the spirits were just confused or didn't understand the term Ho Ho Kam. They might have been answering without understanding just to keep the conversation going. It's possible that spirits from vastly different cultures and times can get together. That's a matter for further research. And we will be back. We will honor our promise and not let these people be forgotten.

The EVPs

DB: Yes.

Did they have horns, what we would call tusks, as large as a man?

Yes.

EVP: Yes.

DB: I think we're in ancient, ancient times.

D: They were Clovis.

To listen to the EVPs go to:

www.beelieveparanormal.com/our-book.html

5

Meanwhile, Back at the Ranch

According to many beliefs and many cultures when we cross over we're allowed to enter a place of joy—the so-called "happy hunting ground" of the Native Americans, for example—Christians have Heaven, Buddhists have Nirvana, and so on. Most people who have passed on had a time, at least a moment, that was for them the happiest time of their lives. That time could be described as "Heaven on Earth." We wondered often if it was possible that someone's "heavenly reward" could be a return to that happy time. In other words, when a person becomes a spirit, are there options?

The exterior of the 96 Ranch ruin.

Dwight and Rhonda outside of the 96 Ranch.

Dan recording EVPs inside the 96 Ranch.

Apparently so. We encountered proof of this somewhat surprising fact on a visit to the 96 Ranch ruin not too far from Florence, Arizona. The property currently has two standing houses (one adobe and one wooden), a large barn, a storage shelter the locals have named "the bomb shelter," a windmill, water tanks, ruined buildings, corrals, and a large barn. Right in the middle of the site is a gray slab of rock sticking only a few inches above the earth. Several grinding holes used by Native Americans were carved into the stone, so obviously the ranch site has been occupied for hundreds and perhaps thousands of years. Our attempts to make contact with the Native Americans were unsuccessful. But the story was quite different when we conducted a session in the nearby barn.

The barn grabbed our attention the minute we entered. Dwight immediately heard faint music. He said it sounded like dance music. Rhonda instantly knew that multiple spirits were around us. The feeling was happy and very upbeat she said. A large, concrete floor was lined with bench seats, which seemed to indicate that the area was used at some times for meetings and get-togethers. As we discovered later, one of those get-togethers was a marriage ceremony, probably followed by a dance and celebration.

After the session we returned to our respective homes and listened to the recordings we had made. One definite EVP proved to be the sound of footsteps. The exploration of the 96 Ranch also proved the value in having multiple witnesses and of double-checking psychic information. That's especially true for EVPs. For example, a review of my recording led me to believe I had captured a very emotional response from a male voice responding to a comment about the happiest moment in a spirit's life on the earthly plane (see following transcript). I could swear I heard "this was my father." When Dwight and Rhonda played the recording on their much more sophisticated audio equipment, they identified the voice as mine saying I had "goose bumps all over." This was disappointing in the sense of not capturing an EVP, but gratifying in that we would not be creating a false contact during research for this book.

The understandable desire to capture a legitimate EVP can easily lead a listener into hearing something that isn't really there. The effect can be compared to seeing familiar objects, persons, or creatures in the shapes formed by clouds. A significant number of probable EVPs were considered for this book, but were ultimately rejected because they fit into the "we're just not 100 percent sure" category.

We sat down on the benches lining the barn and began our session with questions related to the music Dwight was hearing.

D: If there's anybody here who remembers this place as a dance hall or meeting place let us know what your name is and … what's your favorite song here? This might have been somebody's first kiss or first dance.

You know, I just got a feeling … Is there anybody here who got married here?

DB: I think you may have hit on something there.

D: I'm seeing and feeling a wedding situation here.

DB: I got kind of an emotional twinge … a pleasant twinge.

I'm going to place the recorder down … mic down … and get my pendulum out.

Was there ever a wedding held here?

Definitely yes. You nailed it.

D: That's the feeling I get. Somebody's out here with an extremely emotional bond.

DB: Yep. Big strong yes.

Was the wedding held after 1930? Yes.

Was it held after 1940? No.

In the thirties. Was it held in 1935? Just before the war.

D: I was just going to say that's just before the war.

That's kinda' funny because the picture I got was not a "tux 'n tails" kind of wedding. You wear your best Sunday dress.

DB: Your "Sunday go to meeting" clothes.

D: I'm seeing the groom in a brown, kind of a brown suit jacket, but with workpants on. Not really dress pants, but workpants, a white shirt, a black string tie-like is what I'm seeing. I don't see a female, but I see the male.

DB: Was the male who was married a cowhand?

No.

Did the male who was married work at the 96 Ranch?

Yep.

D: To the male who was married, were you related to the people who owned the 96 Ranch?

DB: That's a yes.

D: That's what I thought. I think he's the son of the father ... that's what I'm seeing.

DB: I'm getting a swinging yes ... to your question.

D: If we are talking to the male who got married here, can you tell us your name real quick? I've got a little box here. It's a recorder. It'll record your voice if you come right up to it, come up to us and talk real loud, we can probably hear your voice. If you can tell me your name because I don't like saying "the male" all the time.

R: Tell us what your bride's name is.

D: I'm getting a real strong feeling that this groom went to war and didn't come back.

DB: Did the groom, whatever your name is, fight in World War II? Were you killed in World War II?

That's a yes.

D: That's what I thought. That's what I got.

DB: Were you killed fighting in World War II?

That's a yes.

Were you killed overseas?

Yes.

Were you in the European theater?

That's a no.

Did you fight in the Pacific war theater?

Yes.

R: I'm getting a beach ... killed on a beach.

DB: I'm getting a marine.

D: I think he came back here after because this was—

DB: Probably the last happiest moment of his life.

D: Yes.

R: Ask if his wife's name starts with an "E."

DB: I'm speaking to the groom, did your wife ... did her first name begin with an "E?"

It was going yes even before I finished the question.

R: Because I'm actually seeing her now.

DB: What does she look like?

R: She's about five-seven, five-eight with shoulder-length brown hair, curls. I think she wore a blue dress to the wedding. That's what I'm seeing. I think her name was Evelyn or Evie.

DB: Is Rhonda's description of the bride—

Yes.

Was her name Evie?

No.

Was her name Emily?

I'm getting a yes.

Jumpy pendulum. Lots of energy here.

This was probably his last happy, totally happy memory.

D: Yes. Probably one of the last gatherings before—

R: Big gathering.

D: Signed up. Got married and after that, a few years after that he obviously got shipped off.

DB: They all knew war was coming.

I'm going to end my session.

Regardless of the images and tales told in movies and television, not all so-called haunted houses are filled with demonic and vengeful spirits bent on the terror and destruction of innocents. On the contrary, some haunted houses (or barns) are places of great joy and are filled with happy people having the time of their many lives. Prior to the investigations conducted for this book we would have believed that the marine's spirit, if still earthbound, would have been stuck on that island in the Pacific. He died there tragically and possibly in great shock and pain. Our culture has created the image of ghosts trapped in the place where they died—eternally doomed to relive the last moments of their lives. That is true for *some* spirits, but for others, like the song says, "It ain't necessarily so."

This marine had or was given the choice to return to the earthly plane and that's where he jumped. Instead of reliving a terrible death, he was reliving the happiest moment of his life. He's forever surrounded by friends and family and constantly dancing with the love of his life. Obviously, we didn't attempt to release a spirit who was enjoying such a happy afterlife.

And the dance goes on.

The EVPs

D: I'm seeing the groom in a brown, kind of a brown suit jacket, but with workpants on. Not really dress pants, but workpants, a white shirt, a black string tie-like is what I'm seeing. I don't see a female, but I see the male.

EVP: (Sound of boots with spurs walking across the floor)

To listen to the EVPs go to:

www.beelieveparanormal.com/our-book.html

6

The Flying Nymph Lets Fly

The *New York Times* reported in 1882 that "the Bird Cage Theater is the Wildest, Wickedest Night Spot, Between Basin Street and the Barbary Coast." In other words, you couldn't find a more interesting, challenging, and dangerous saloon between New Orleans and San Francisco during Tombstone's brief, but famous heyday. The theater was active 24 hours a day 365 days a year, from 1881 through 1889. A lot of that action involved gunplay. Today the guides will point out some of the more than 140 bullet holes scattered throughout the building. Many of them are in the roof of the main gallery, although you can find some frighteningly near the stage.

The exterior of the Bird Cage Theater in Tombstone, Arizona, circa 1940. Courtesy Library of Congress.

Entertainment was provided by top-of-the-line troops and personalities, including Lizette, "the Flying Nymph" who flew from one side of the theatre to the other on a rope. The famous belly dancer Fatima donated a painting of herself that still hangs in the lobby. The canvas has six bullet holes and a knife slash in it. Comedian Eddy Foy appeared around the time of the infamous gunfight at the OK Corral. Following the performances the house orchestra would play from an orchestra pit until sunrise. Dancing girls performed and sold drinks, and in many cases, sex. Fourteen private boxes on two balconies overlooked the hall and the stage. Whiskey, beer, and cigars were delivered upstairs by a dumbwaiter at the end of the bar. Each cage featured drapes that could be closed when the prostitutes got down to business.

A poker room was located in the basement and was the site of the longest-running poker game in history—24 hours a day for eight years. Participants included Doc Holliday, Bat Masterson, Diamond Jim Brady, George Hearst, and Adolphus Busch. Visitors say they sometimes hear the sound of cards being shuffled and chips being tossed on the table, often to the distant sound of music popular in the late 1800s. Two elaborate rooms across the narrow hall were used by the more upscale hostesses.

The Bird Cage's run of luck ran out when the Tombstone mines flooded and could no longer produce the silver that created the boomtown. The dramatic loss of business almost, but not quite, killed the "town too tough to die."

Dwight lived in Tombstone for fourteen years and became close to many of the employees working at the theatre, now a major tourist attraction. He also became acquainted with some of the patrons who lived, played, and died during the glory days. A visit to the Bird Cage Theater for us was mandatory. We conducted sessions behind the stage, in the basement near the poker room, and in the shop. Despite the constant music blaring over the facility's loudspeakers and the occasional interruption from tourists, we were able to make contact. We even met Lizette, who let fly some strong opinions about some of the other late residents.

D: Okay, We're rolling. Session two, Birdcage Theater. We're going to do a pendulum session here in the gift shop.

(**NOTE:** Rhonda stopped at a back wall, which featured photos of prostitutes and entertainers who performed at the old Bird Cage. One of those photos was of Lizette, the Flying Nymph. Dwight shot video of the session.)

D: I want to document this.

DB: Are there any spirits with us right now.

R: Yes there are.

DB: I get a big yes.

Is there somebody named Rebecca here?

She's not here.

R: Is Lizette here?

DB: Big yes.

DB/EVP (?): Which Lizette?

DB/EVP (?): Uhh …

The Flying Nymph.

R: Lizette, do you remember Dwight and myself?

Because I remember talking to you before.

DB: Oh, yeah. Big swing yes.

R: I think we talked to you before. I think we have video of you trying to talk to us.

Yep. It always helps to put a face to who you see.

DB: Beautiful girl.

R: Thank you.

DB: We'd appreciate it if you'd say something.

R: Did you ever use the name Rebecca? When you were here?

DB: I get a no.

R: No.

Do you know who Rebecca is?

DB: I'm getting a yes.

R: Okay. Well, please tell her hello from the girl upstairs...

(**NOTE:** The female attendant/guide in the lobby had mentioned her frequent encounters with a red-headed woman from the 1800s named Rebecca.)

DB: She's saying no.

R: Do you guys not get along?

DB: Rephrase that.

R: Do you get along with Rebecca?

DB: No.

R: No.

Was Rebecca judgmental?

DB: Yes.

R: Okay. Rebecca was a performer? Was she a performer?

DB: No!

R: Was she a prostitute?

DB: Yes.

R: Yes. She thought she was better than you. Did she think she was better than everybody … okay? That's what I thought. That was the impression I got.

DB: I'm getting a yes.

R: Okay. I won't ask you to say hello then.

DB: Okay!

R: (laughs) So, have you met Leroy?

DB: Powerful yes.

(**NOTE:** Leroy was a recent employee at the Bird Cage Theater and a friend to Dwight and Rhonda. He passed away some years ago, but he still hangs out at the theater.)

R: Can you tell him hello from us, from Dwight and I. We used to see him all the time. Thank you.

And tell him we miss seeing him at WalMart. We used to see him at the store.

DB: Pretty strong feeling there.

R: Do you and Leroy get along well? That's what I thought.

DB: Are you here because you want to be here?

That's a yes.

Could you be someplace else if you wanted to be?

That's a yes.

Are you here in our present and your past at the same time—or your present at the same time?

That's the second time that's happened. You know, they're in both time frames because I'm getting a strong yes.

R: Right.

That was weird. That was so weird. Is the air blowing? I guess it's possible, but I've just seen this wiggling just a minute ago. It was like all over the place wiggling.

(**NOTE:** Reference is to tablecloth draped over a display table that was blowing as if in the wind. Observed by all three. The doors to the gift shop were shut at that time.)

DB: Maybe somebody opened the door.

R: Well, maybe it could have been, but that was kind of crazy.

DB: She's talking about a tablecloth.

R: Are there any … do you know if there are any children that play here?

Not right now.

DB: That's a no.

R: Do you see this place as it was when you were here?

DB: Yes.

And do you see it as it is now?

That's a yes.

R: Are there a lot of spirits with you as well?

DB: That's the strongest yes we've had.

R: Are there still spirits playing cards and doing what they did when the Birdcage was open?

DB: Yes.

I'm getting some of the strongest pendulum movements I've ever gotten in any of our investigations.

R: Yes. It's pretty strong here.

DB: Are you happy here?

Yes.

Could you be someplace else if you wanted to be?

Yes.

R: Yes. They want to be here.

Did you enjoy being here when you were … yeah.

DB: A wide swing. Look at that.

R: Do you want to ask anything, Dwight?

D: No. I'm doing some clearing actually so we've got video of this, which will work out good.

DB: I'm not doing that. (Reference to wide pendulum swing)

D: There's nobody to help.

R: Yeah, there's nobody here to help.

DB: Ask that directly.

R: Is there anybody here that needs help?

DB: Nope. Neat. Is there anything else we need to do?

I'm serious this is the most powerful pendulum swing in any of our ...

R: Strongest.

D: You get some real ... I got that on video.

DB: (reference to pendulum swing) I'm not doing that.

R: Do people stop to talk to you often?

DB: No. She's leaving.

R: Well, we'll come back and talk to you later.

DB: It's dropping out of my hand. There we go. She's gone. That was neat.

R: Yes, it was.

D: We got some really good video when you were asking questions. You could see the ...

DB: That was ... normally you get a good swing every once in a while and a moderate swing. This was all wide swings, which is unusual.

Well, this is ending the EVP session. This is your last chance to speak up.

It's interesting that feelings about other people, places, and things are carried on or can be carried on once someone has passed. Lizette's feelings about Rebecca bear this out. Lizette also provided confirmation of a theme running through many of our sessions. Many spirits haunt a place because they make a conscious choice to be in that place. It's also interesting that the spirit isn't trapped unaware. As Lizette said, she could see the Bird Cage as it was and as it is. For whatever reason, the Bird Cage Theatre was and is a place where she and other spirits are ... happy.

The EVPs

Dwight lived in Tombstone 15 years and one of his relationships was with a fellow named Caleb, who has since crossed over. Caleb showed up during an EVP session recorded before *Time Served*.

Woman: The man who did the lecture?

Caleb: Now, who gives a shit.

Dwight: If you hadn't have asked, I coulda' told ya.'

Sources for additional reading on the Birdcage Theater:

The Official Birdcage Theater Site:
  tombstonebirdcage.com

Desert Honkytonk by Roger A. Bruns

The Bird Cage Theater: A Guide to Legends, Artifacts and Ghosts by Charles William Edelman.

To listen to the EVPs go to:

www.beelieveparanormal.com/our-book.html

7

Making Friends at Fairbank

Paranormal investigators can make friends and establish relationships with those who have crossed. Several spirits in different locations expressed a willingness to engage in further contact. People who were outgoing and friendly on this side seem to be the same way on the other side. How do we know? The spirits said so.

A little girl afraid to cross over hangs out with the spirits of other children, but casts a lonely eye across the veil to the family she wants to join. We encountered this spirit at Fairbank ghost town. We wondered about the force that kept her on this side. We also wondered if we could help her rejoin her family. On the same trip we met the spirit of a miner taking it easy at his house across from the mill. He appeared to be someone perfectly content to remain right where he was.

ARIZ., 2. FAIRB, 1-5   HABS

The Fairbank Hotel, circa 1937. Courtesy Library of Congress.

We had come to Fairbank prepared to do whatever we could to help any spirit in need of help. We had been instrumental in helping others cross over to a better life after death. We were surprised on this venture when we met spirits who didn't want or need any help. Does a paranormal investigator even have the right to try to ease someone over to the other side when that person just doesn't want to go?

These are two of the spirits we encountered on our visit. The experience was as rewarding as it was puzzling. And our education into the workings of the spirit world continued—as did our growing list of questions about those workings.

Fairbank on the San Pedro River is one of the best-preserved ghost towns, and one of the easiest to access; it is about ten miles west of Tombstone. Fairbank is located in a lovely spot and because it is close to the river it's quite lush, especially after the Arizona rains. In contrast to the mesquite- and cactus-studded Chihuahuan Desert surrounding it, the small town features large trees and shaded pathways. Originally, the area was part of a Spanish Land Grant known as the San Juan de las Boquillas y Nogales grant. The town was founded in 1881 as Junction City. The name was changed to Kendall when it became a stage stop on the road to Tombstone. Later the name was changed to Fairbank, after N. K. Fairbank, a Chicago financier who funded much of the town's development, including the nearby Grand Central Mill, a large ruin in much worse shape than the nearby town. Still, the mill is an impressive site dominating the once-bustling community.

Fairbank was the nearest railhead to the famous "town too tough to die," Tombstone, which at the time was one of the largest cities in the West, with a population of more than 15,000 residents. Fairbank's population was about 100 served by a Wells Fargo office, five saloons, four stores, three restaurants, a hotel, a school, and a jail. Most of the residents worked for the Central Mining Company's Grand Central Mill or for the railroad. Four different railroads were served by three depots. The mill's ten stamps ran 24 hours a day seven days a week and the constant booming of the machinery could be heard for miles in all directions. This goes a long way toward explaining the need for so many saloons.

Fairbank folded and cashed in most of its few remaining chips not too long after its founding, suffering from a double whammy of financial misfortune. The mines in Tombstone flooded, which closed them down and slowly the other mining operations failed or became too costly to continue operations. With no ore to process there was no longer a need for the mill or mill workers. As the number of jobs dwindled so did Fairbank's population. At the same time the area's farmers suffered from a drought, further aggravating the small community's financial woes. A flood in 1890 pretty much finished off Fairbank.

Some of those residents haven't given up on the old rail-head yet and still wander the streets that are empty except for the occasional tourist, history buff, or paranormal investigator.

We arrived on a very hot July morning to an empty parking lot and a day full of promise. A number of well-preserved buildings provided a look at what the business end of town was like during its heyday. The area where the people lived across the highway is now little more than a series of rubble piles. A narrow trail out of the town plaza led about a quarter of a mile to the cemetery, which is located on top of a rocky hill, offering a beautiful view of the surrounding landscape. Like the town, Fairbank's cemetery has seen better days—much better days. Unlike the town, the cemetery is slowly being reclaimed by the desert. Iron-work, crumbling brick structures, rock outlines, and crude and broken crosses mark a hilltop being taken over by scrub brush, desert flowers, and weeds.

Rhonda's intuition directed us to a section they named the "family grave site" on a previous visit. It's a multiple burial protected by an ornate wire fence anchored by heavy iron bars. There are no headstones or identifications of who lies beneath, but clearly the interred were people of some prominence. We sat down among the scurrying ants and began our first session of the day.

D: Good morning to whoever is out here with us. We came out to talk to you to see if you're wanting to talk to us this morning. We have two devices out here. They're voice recorders. They will record your voice, which means we can play back later and hopefully hear what you have to say. And also our friend Dan here has a pendulum and I'm pretty sure you know what that is. So, we're just going to do a little bit of a Q&A session here and talk to you a little bit. Please, please feel free to talk to us at any time, interact with us at any time. That's what we're here for.

Let me start off easy by asking is there anyone here with us this morning?

DB: Okay, I'm getting a yes. And I asked earlier, before we started, and I got a yes.

D: Okay. Good.

R: Are there any children here with us?

DB: Strong yes. I think there's more than one.

R: Yeah. I do, too. I already knew that. I just wanted your confirmation there.

Is there a little girl here with us?

DB: A good, solid yes.

D: One of the last times I was here I heard a voice of a little girl saying, "Help me." Is that you?

DB: Yes.

D: Okay, well, we are here to try to do that if that is something you want us to do.

R: Do you still need help?

DB: Yes.

D: Do you need help to try to get away from here?

DB: That's a pretty solid yes.

D: We can try to help you with that. That's one of the things we do.

R: Honey, do you need help finding your family?

DB: I'm getting a yes.

D: Do you know if your family may have crossed over and went to the other side?

DB: No.

D: Okay.

R: No her family didn't go or no she doesn't know?

D: She doesn't know.

R: I think they did.

DB: I get a confirmation on what you just said.

R: I think they went over and somehow you got confused and didn't make it over with them?

DB: That's another yes.

D: You know or I guess I'll let you know that you can cross over at any time you want to. Did you know that you could cross over?

DB: That's a strong yes.

R: Well, your family is right over there, honey. They're over there waiting for you.

DB: She knows. I'm getting a yes.

R: Do you want to go over there?

DB: Yeah, that's a yes. A weak yes, but it was a yes.

R: Do you enjoy playing here with the other kids?

DB: That's a strong yes.

D: I was going to ask if there was something keeping her here, but that pretty much answered my question.

R: Why don't you take the other kids who are here and help them cross over?

DB: I got a no on that.

R: No.

You can come back. Do you know that?

DB: I'm getting neutral. My interpretation is that it means confusion, but that's what I'm getting. Neutral.

R: Once you find your family you can come back and play with the kids. Did you know that?

DB: Yes.

R: Okay. I just wanted to make sure.

D: You have to be ready to go.

R: Are you ready to go?

DB: Yes. I got a definite feeling of yes before the pendulum even started swinging.

D: Yes.

R: I think you should go into the light or whatever you see to cross over. Go find your mom and dad and your siblings. Then when you want to come back you can do that.

DB: I'm getting a good solid yes. I stopped it and let it start again and I got another yes.

R: When you come back just make sure you tell your parents so they know where to wait for you, honey.

DB: I think she's going.

D: Maybe she just needed an adult to give her permission.

R: I think she was confused that she wasn't going to be able to find her parents and then come back. It was like going to a friend's house and then trying to find your way home. That's the type of feeling I was getting.

DB: This is interesting. I was getting the feeling that she was fading and the pendulum circle kept getting smaller and smaller and smaller and it just started slipping out of my hand.

D: Interesting.

DB: But the circle went down from about a three-inch circumference to a pinpoint circle ... just a slow, slow winding down.

R: Yeah, she didn't ...

DB: Flash out.

R: Right.

DB: Like at Tombstone. (Reference to an earlier session)

R: Right.

DB: And that was instantaneous.

R: She just kinda' moseyed away.

DB: Mosey is a better word than faded.

D: Hopefully she made it.

R: I think she found her parents. That's what she was afraid of—not being able to find them—and then come back ... so, that's why I said plan with them where to meet them when you want to come back.

DB: Well, I just asked if the little girl is still here and I got a no. That may be wishful thinking on my part, but that was a definite no.

R: I definitely think she went.

DB: I think so. I felt … moseyed is a better word than fading.

R: It's almost as if she skipped over.

D: Yep.

DB: There was a definite shift in pendulum movement. I'll show you. (demonstrating) Slowly, slowly, slowly, but I'm controlling that. But it was a lot smoother than I'm making it. But it was a lot smoother than what I just did.

R: It was kinda' like when you were a kid and you have your kids wait on the front porch to watch you when you went somewhere. It was almost like that … as if she wanted us to watch her so she would be safe … in case she got lost. Does that make any sense?

DB: Look at this. I just asked my High Self if we just helped somebody cross over. Look how wide that's spinning.

D: Yeah. That's wide. That's a big yes.

That's one of those not real dramatic …

DB: It doesn't have to be dramatic.

R: It wasn't emotional, but she definitely needed some grownups to help her with direction.

DB: I'm wondering if there's anyone here who saw that happen if they would like to say something about that.

D: You can come here and tell us. If you saw that happen. Can you tell us if we're right? Did the girl cross over to the other side?

DB: It would help us with confirmation. We have what's best for her at heart.

R: Why are you here? Why are you still here?

D: If you wanted to leave, if you did see the little girl go you can follow her and go to the same place if that's what you want. (pause) I have to say if you're going to stay somewhere, this isn't a bad place to have beautiful scenery to look out at. We will be here for a while today. We're going to leave here. We're going to walk down to the Grand Central Mill. You're welcome to come with us.

And if you did talk to us hopefully our little recorders picked that up. And if you did talk to us we can always come back and talk to you again if you'd like to.

R: Did you live in town?

D: A lot of bird sounds today.

D: Yeah.

R: A lot of nature sounds for sure.

I feel like there's a man here as well. I don't know what you guys are picking up.

DB: That's what I'm getting. Almost like a caretaker.

R: Yep.

DB: But not of the cemetery, but more of a caretaker of who's here.

R: Like a caretaker of the spirits. And I feel like he was kind of a rancher guy, a ... not a miner, just a very laid back ...

DB: I just got an impression, for what it's worth, that he's here out of choice.

R: Yeah. I think that's right, Dan.

DB: Well, I think we did what we set out to do. I hope.

D: We at least got something, maybe.

We appreciate you talking with us if you did. We appreciate you allowing us to share your space. As I said, we're going to head down to the Grand Central. If you want to, come along.

We walked on an elevated stretch of land, the old road above the lower riverbed, under a canopy of shade, which provided a welcome respite from the increasing heat of the day. In an earlier visit Dwight noticed an area with spotty growth broken by small plots of bare earth. He thought that might be the location of a residence or support facility for the mill. We examined the area and found his speculation right on target. The area was littered with old refuse and trash. Except for the ubiquitous modern beer or soda can, all the trash was tossed during the days when the mill was in operation. We found a fairly cleared area and began our second session of the day.

D: We are directly across from the Grand Central Mill site at the "cabin" site.

DB: It's a rather warm day.

D: We are here and we hope that there are people with us here now. We like to preserve history and that's what we're trying to do here.

DB: Let me tell you how this works. I just asked my pendulum, "Are there people here" and got a yes.

D: Okay.

DB: We're the three people here? So you have to ask if there are spirits here.

D: Yeah.

DB: That's why you have to be careful when you ask questions and use a pendulum.

R: Yeah.

D: Right.

DB: Because I'm thinking one thing and I'm asking something entirely different.

D: True. True.

D: So there is…

DB: Spirits here.

D: Spirits here other than us?

Are you a male?

DB: That's a yes.

D: That's what I thought.

DB: Is there more than one spirit here? I'm getting a no.

D: Okay, so there's just one male.

Well, good afternoon, sir. We thank you for allowing us to be here. Were you a worker at the mill across the way?

DB: Yes.

(Sound—loud pop)

R: That was a water bottle.

DB: Water bottle I think. Curious timing, though.

D: Did you die working at the mill?

DB: No.

R: Did you have … did you get a disease?

DB: Yes.

R: Did you have tuberculosis?

DB: Neutral. He may not know what that is. Consumption.

R: Do you have consumption?

DB: Yes.

D: Let me ask you, sir, to help with this consumption, did you drink a lot of bitters?

DB: Yes. Fast yes.

R: You might note that you're (Dwight) sniffing a lot. Just for the recorders.

D: We did find a lot of … found a bottle out here, in fact out there, that was bitters so we figured it might be used for medicinal purposes. Is that true?

DB: He was swinging yes.

D: Well, sir, sorry to hear that. Are you happy staying here?

DB: A good, firm yes.

R: It is pretty out here.

D: It's beautiful out here. You've got a really good private area here.

R: Hotter than hell, but it's pretty.

DB: Was it hot for you?

No.

D: Good.

R: That's good to know.

DB: Are you alone?

I'm getting a yes.

R: Do other people visit you on the other side?

DB: Rephrase that.

R: Do people come back here to be with you? Do they come back to this place?

DB: Yes. Yes. That was me both times.

R: That's good to know.

DB: Didn't mean to step on you. (Audio reference.)

R: No, that's fine.

D: Allergies are killing me out here.

R: Did you have allergies when you were alive?

DB: Yeah.

R: They're really pretty bad out here.

Were you married?

DB: That's a yes.

D: Did your wife leave here before you did.

DB: Strong no.

D: Okay, so she stayed. Stayed here with you. That's good.

DB: I'm curious. Did you die at this location? Where we are?

DB: That's a yes.

D: Is there anything that you left behind? Let me rephrase that. It was kind of a general question.

DB: But I was getting a yes answer.

R: Did you leave all your possessions behind here?

DB: No.

R: Maybe, did you leave a couple of trunks or footlockers.

DB: Fast yes.

(Dwight picks up a modern plastic hair comb.)

R: Is that your comb?

D: I doubt it. It's plastic.

R: I'm being a smart ass. Thank you for having a sense of humor.

DB: Was your nickname "Ace."

D: Yeah …

(much laughing)

Sir, I'll ask you, you lived right across from the mill. Was it extremely loud all the time?

DB: That's the strongest yes so far.

D: I can imagine. I don't know how you slept.

R: Maybe they were just so tired from working they could sleep through that noise somehow.

D: I'm thinking a little liquid libation was probably some sleeping tonic.

R: Yeah.

DB: I'm getting a big yes.

D: Yes, sir. I understand completely.

DB: So you're perfectly content to stay here?

That's a yes.

D: That's great. I hope you're happy. We really appreciate you allowing us to talk, to communicate with you today. Would you like us to come back some time and talk to you again?

DB: Immediate yes.

D: Okay. We will certainly do that. We live near here. Dan came a lot further, but we can always make that trip.

DB: It's a powerful yes.

R: We live over by Tombstone by Fort Huachuca.

D: Well, sir, I'm going to close it down. It's getting kind of hot for us. I know it's hot for you, but I do want to thank you for being here with us and talking with us. And we will be back sir. Thank you again.

DB: We do appreciate it.

R: Nice to meet you.

D: End of EVP session two.

So, what was the bottom line to our effort? Emotionally and psychically we each believed we had made contact with the little girl and the miner. As usual, there is no way to prove it, but we firmly believe we helped the girl cross over and at last rejoin her family.

When and if we can, we try to help those spirits cross over who want to make that journey. Occasionally we encounter someone who can't be helped or who refuses for whatever reason to be helped.

And we occasionally encounter someone who is perfectly happy to remain where he or she is. It seems to us that sometimes a spirit returns to a place of happiness and contentment or where he feels he belongs. This was the case with the miner, and in this situation we did not feel right in trying to encourage him in a path he so obviously didn't want to take.

So, bottom line—we've made a new friend, someone from the other side. We'll be back from time to time just to say hello. We think he'll like that. And we always appreciate good company.

Readers interested in Fairbank history can find good information at:

www.arizonaghosttowntrails.com/fairbank.html

www.ghosttownaz.info/fairbank-ghost-town.php

8

A Strike-Out and a Home Run at Sasco

Actual paranormal investigation isn't nearly as dramatic *all the time* as is often depicted on television and in other media. People doing this type of work for very long inevitably experience times in which they do not get a response from the other side. The reasons are varied.

Ghosts have schedules too. It's likely that in some of our investigations we have shown up when there was nobody home. The energy on the other side wasn't sufficient for a message to cross over to us. The spirits weren't in a talkative mood. As Dwight has pointed out, personalities may not change just because someone has crossed over. A shy person on this side of the line may be just as shy on the other side.

The ruins of the Sasco Rockland Hotel.

More ruins of the Sasco Rockland Hotel.

He, she, or they just might not have anything to say.

The spirit might be a jerk.

The investigator came calling when no one was home.

Sasco, a milling community, is located between Phoenix and Tucson and was named for the Southern Arizona Smelter Company. Just after the turn of the twentieth century the town had a population of 600. The smelter, which processed ore (primarily copper) from the nearby Silverbell and a dozen or so other mines in the area, was active from 1907 until 1910, although the post office remained open until 1919. Today, the smelter site is substantial and consists of numerous buildings in surprisingly good condition for a ghost town/operation. Unfortunately, much of the site has been taken over and trashed by the paintball, spray paint, and party crowd.

Across the access road to the mill is the old town site. All that remains are the remnants of old walls, some concrete flooring here and there, large holes that were probably cellars, and piles of junk more than a century old. A substantial and well-built cellar or basement is located down from the town and we speculated that it was used to hold explosives. While walking through one of the numerous junk piles Rhonda found a perfectly preserved 1907 liberty head nickel. So, apparently there is still treasure to be found in old Sasco. Just east of the facility are the walls of the Rockland Hotel, built for overnight guests doing business at the mill.

One of the structures in the town site, just the foundation of walls and some flooring, was rather large for the community and contained a number of smaller rooms. Dwight guessed that the building had been a hospital or medical facility. The layout and some of the rusted artifacts scattered about supported the theory. We thought we'd see if we could capture any EVPs. Unfortunately, we just plain struck out. The session is included here just to provide insight into how paranormal investigations works—and sometimes didn't work. The transcript indicates how often natural sounds interfere with an EVP recording. Wise investigators identify those sounds as they occur so that later they don't mistake them for the real thing when reviewing the recordings.

The session following was much longer than the transcript indicates because we often paused for some time to allow spirits time to respond or to make their own comments. Sometimes we would even leave the recorders going for a few moments after ending a session just on the hope that we'll get a "goodbye" or "come back and see us."

D: Okay, EVP session two in Sasco. It is 10:01 a.m. August 1 (Rhonda in background w/water bottle.)

We are in a building of some sort. We do not know what it is, just yet.

DB: It is substantial.

D: It is big. We think it is either some kind of a store or maybe even some kind of a medical unit … hospital, that kind of thing.

Let me start off. Is there anybody with us right now who would like to speak to us?

If there are people here with us or a person with us, we do ask if you'd like to step up close to us and tell us your name very loudly so you can be heard.

R: Is there somebody here who was shot?

(Background breathing, probably DB who was holding recorder close because of the wind.)

D: We're curious if this is a medical building. If not, can you tell us what this building was used for?

R: How old are you? Just for the record I'm picking up 45-ish.

D: This was an awfully big building. It looks like different rooms or sub-buildings on the outside. It had a concrete floor.

R: There are flies flying around, too.

DB: Airplane noise in the background.

Did anybody die in this building?

D: That was my stomach.

DB: Again we'd like to know what this structure was all about if you could tell us.

D: Well, that's good enough for me. If anybody was going to talk they would have done it.

DB: Okay. Appreciate it.

D: End EVP session two.

All we got during that brief session was a hyperactive bee, a gurgling stomach, and heavy breathing from holding a recorder too close to the love handles. And that's how it sometimes goes. The key for us is the realization that there are still spirits about and that a strike out at one site just means it's time to move onto another.

A Change of Luck with the Flip of a Coin

We moved over to what we assumed was the hospital or clinic for the community. Here we encountered an enlightening spirit whose schedule permitted him time to interact with three paranormal investigators.

There wasn't much at the location except the remnants of four walls—and that 1907 liberty head nickel Rhonda had discovered. We decided to hold a full session. Finding that coin seemed to be more than just a coincidence, at least that's the way we felt about it. It is certainly possible that the coin was put in place by the action of a spirit wanting to communicate. It's equally possible that it showed up as a result of wind and rain and good luck. Either way, we took the find as a good omen and we decided to proceed immediately. That site and the spirit there produced one of the most interesting sessions recorded for this book.

One of the most fascinating areas we've investigated is the nature of the other side. What is it like over there? Who's there? What happens when you cross over? Are matters set in stone or does the individual spirit have choices? What is the nature of "haunting"?

That list of 501 questions grows in length at virtually every investigation. The spirit encountered in Sasco provided some fascinating insights into this complex subject.

D: EVP session one at Sasco town site. We're at a building, rubble of a building. It is August 1 at 9:23 in the morning and we just found a coin at this site, so we're going to stop and do a quick EVP session. I'm setting the recorder down and [am now] hands free. So, is there anybody with us today who wants to talk to us? I mean you can talk to us. We've got these little things we're talking into and we can record your voice, and we'll be able to hear it later.

We appreciate you allowing us to be out here today.

R: How many people are here today with us?

DB: I'm getting more than one.

R: Are there two people here?

DB: Yes.

R: Are there more than two people here?

DB: No.

R: Okay, thank you. Is there a female here, a woman?

DB: That's a good yes.

R: And are you with a male?

DB: Strong yes.

R: Thank you.

D: I'm speaking to the male, did you work at the mills here in Sasco?

DB: Yes.

D: To the woman who is here, if you can tell us your name that would be great for recording purposes. For the woman here, did you like it in this area?

DB: Yes.

(To Rhonda) Are you getting the same feeling?

R: Yes. I'm getting the same feeling.

D: Yeah, if they're still here I'd have to say they liked it here.

R: Did you like Arizona, this territory?

DB: Big strong yes.

R: Are you from the East Coast?

DB: Yes.

R: That's what I was feeling … better weather out here, maybe.

DB: Yes.

R: That's how I feel too.

D: This place where we're at right now, this patch of ground, was this your house?

DB: Powerful yes.

D: Okay.

R: To you, in your dimension, does your house look like it did when you were living in this dimension?

DB: I was swinging yes halfway through your question.

R: Okay. Thank you. I wondered about that and I thought that was correct even though in this realm the house doesn't exist anymore.

Is it nice over there where you are?

DB: That's the biggest yes so far.

R: Is it beautiful over there? Is it what you expected?

DB: No.

R: So, it isn't what you expected?

DB: Ask that in another way.

R: Is the afterlife or heaven what you expected?

DB: Again, no.

R: Is it beautiful over there?

DB: Yes.

R: Again, thank you for your confirmation. That's everything that I've been told and what I felt, but it's nice to have validation, so I appreciate that.

DB: Let me ask a question. Did you choose to live in that dimension in this time in this place as it appears in your dimension?

That's a yes.

So, this is a choice?

Yes again.

R: So from what I understand, when you cross over to the afterlife it's a choice in what you do?

DB: Immediate yes.

R: Okay. We always have a choice even after we leave our physical body. Is that correct?

R: Thank you.

DB (simultaneously): Yes.

D: You said it wasn't what you expected. Is it better on the other side where you're at than what you expected?

DB: That's a yes.

D: Well, that's good to know. I'm happy for you, it's good to know that it's better than you expected.

R: Was life hard for you when you were here and living?

DB: Yes.

R: Well, we found some of your money and we're going to treasure it and save it for you ... to preserve it.

DB: Is there something you'd like to say to us other than just answering yes or no questions? Go ahead and say so.

I'd like to give them an opportunity to say something.

D: Absolutely. As I said, we do have these little boxes here that'll record your voice if you talk really loud and clear.

R: Did they have any recording device back in the early 1900s?

D: The only thing they had back then was the old turn/crank record players and those ... only if you were extremely wealthy, but it's the same idea.

R: Yeah.

DB: Speaking to the male, were you a manager of some type at the mill?

I got a yes.

R: It's really beautiful out here. Did you guys have a problem with Indians at all when you were out here?

DB: No.

R: Did you have a problem with bad characters when you were out here?

DB: That's a yes.

R: There's always going to be those kinds of people.

DB: The two of you are happy here, yes or no?

I get a moderate yes.

D: Well, I'm glad for you. I'm happy that you guys are happy here. Definitely could be worse places to be.

R: Absolutely.

DB: It's gorgeous.

D: It's beautiful scenery. It's a gorgeous spot. Nice and quiet.

DB: Is it quiet in your dimension?

No.

D: Do you still see the town, the whole town, as it was when you were alive here?

DB: Yes.

D: Ah, yes.

DB: The mill's running. It would be loud.

D: Almost … not so much a dimensional thing as you know a time warp thing. So, just so I'm clear, everything around you is the same way it was when you were alive?

DB: Yes.

D: That's interesting.

R: Is it that way everywhere in your dimension,.. that everything exists as it did when you were living...? No.

DB: Big no.

R: Okay.

DB: Let me ask a simple question. Did you ever live in the dimension where we are living now?

Yes. So, they're a crossover.

R: Is it a choice to go places that were exactly as you left them in this world.

DB: Yes.

R: It's kinda' like a Star Trek episode where you go into ... what's the alternate reality ... where they ... never mind ... I know what I'm thinking; I just can't get it out.

DB: Well, it's clear they have choices.

D: Let me ask to the woman, and I really do thank you for talking with us so much this morning. We're talking about your reality and ours here now. Did you have a choice as to what time period you could go to?

DB: I get a yes.

D: Interesting. So, it's almost like time traveling. Could you have gone back in time farther if you wanted to?

DB: That's a yes.

D: Interesting.

R: Can you go forward in time?

DB: No.

D: That's even more interesting.

DB: I have a question. In your choices, were they limited to life experiences that you have had—maybe I'm talking reincarnation, perhaps—were your choices always limited to your experiences, your personal experiences?

I get a yes.

D: So long as we're on that subject, do you … okay, let me think how to word this. I don't want to get too complicated.

DB: Quantum mechanics here.

D: Yeah. Now that you're in the other dimension and you chose to be where you're at now are you aware that you lived in other times?

DB: Yes.

R: So is your reincarnated past … are you told about your past in different lives?

DB: Yes. Yes.

R: Wow! That adds a new spin.

D: That adds a whole new spin. Just so I'm clear, you had a choice to go back to that time period that you are in right now.

DB: Yes.

D: Very interesting. Thank you so much for ... I mean that's ...

R: That's a whole world of information.

D: I don't know if you're breaking any rules over there for telling us this, but we sure appreciate it.

R: While we're on that subject, is there any type of manual you get when you cross over? Or rules?

DB: No.

You're watching too many movies.

(Laughter)

R: Well, it's interesting because people ask this question. Paranormal investigators have been asking and you don't get many answers. The spirits are tight-lipped or maybe it's just the spirits you run into who are tight-lipped. It's almost like *Quantum Leap* or whatever that show was.

DB: Maybe they think we're not ready to handle that information. I mean a lot of people can't.

R: That's true.

DB: Let me get this straight. You could have chosen any time period in which you have lived before. Is that correct?

I get a yes.

R: Wow.

D: That is interesting. Thank you so much.

R: That is so ... this is all going in a book, so we appreciate you talking to us.

DB: That's why we'd love to hear your name.

R: We're here to learn, but we're also here to enlighten others on what we learn. We just put that information out there and people can do what they want.

D: Ma'am, I'm speaking to the female here, because you've given us so much great information, can you please ... if you can step up to me and just very loudly and clearly if you can just tell me your name, your first name ... because we'd really love to have your name in our book.

R: You've been just a world of help.

D: Sir, if you're still with us, if you could tell us your name as well, that would be fantastic.

Okay, I have no more questions. That's pretty much ...

R: That's pretty mind blowing. That's a lot to absorb.

D: That's given me a whole lot of thinking there.

R: No wonder people don't do a lot of ... 'cause that's ...

DB: Again, is there anything you'd like to say because we'd love to hear it.

R: We do and we can certainly come back out and talk to you. We don't live very far away, any of us.

D: Well, again, thank you.

DB: Thank you.

R: Yeah, thank you so much.

D: We'll stop bothering you for now. We're going to be out there for a while. If you can or if you would like to you're more than welcome to come along.

R: Point out something. Get our attention.

D: Once again, we thank you for allowing us to be in your home, in your space. Thank you again for talking to us and giving us such incredible information.

R: And helping us find something that belonged to you.

DB: Nice touch.

D: Okay picking up recorder. Ending EVP session one.

You Can't Get Rum 'n' Coke in Charleston

We had visited this grassy, brush- and scrub brush-covered maze of crumbling adobe structures several times. We spoke with a number of spirits including Jack the bartender, and a boarding house operator named Mary, who was also the victim of a modern-day murder. An interesting conversation occurred between Rhonda and Jack and spanned the 150-year history of the Charleston, Arizona ghost town when she "ordered" a rum and coke in the hope of getting an EVP response. Seconds later she discovered why you can't get rum 'n' coke in the Charleston ghost town.

Rhonda and Dwight near the ruins in Charleston, Arizona.

Charleston is rapidly losing its battle with encroaching desert growth, erosion by rain, and washouts from the San Pedro River. During its brief heyday the community was home to 450 people. Most of them worked at or in some way supported the operations of the Tombstone Mill and Mining Company, a ten-stamp mill, the Corbin Mill and Mining Company's fifteen-stamp mill, and the Tombstone Mine and Milling Co., which were all located across the river on the east side. These mills operated around the clock every day of the year. Charleston was a "bedroom community" for Millville. Both communities were dependent upon the silver ore shipped in from the mines in nearby Tombstone. By 1879 more than 40 buildings housed a post office, four restaurants, a school, a church, a doctor, a lawyer, a drugstore, two blacksmiths, two livery stables, two butcher shops, two bakeries, a hotel, five general stores, a jewelry shop, a brickyard, a brewery, a carpenter shop, a drugstore, one doctor, two bakeries, a lawyer, a washhouse, a stationery and fruit store, a brickyard, and at least four saloons.

The community was named after the town's first postmaster, Charles D. Handy.

Charleston was popular with the "cowboy" contingent of the Earp/Clanton conflict made famous in such movies as *Tombstone* and *Wyatt Earp*. Frank Stillwell, killed by Wyatt Earp in Tucson, owned a bar in Charleston. The Clanton Ranch was only a few miles south of town. Some of the cowboys who visited the town included Ike and Billy Clanton, John Ringo, Curly Bill Brocius, Pete Spence, and Frank and Tom McLaury. Despite the rough nature of some residents and frequent guests, the *Tombstone Epitaph* of May 6, 1882, noted, "The town is well regulated and free from turmoil. In fact, it is one of the most peaceful places we were ever in."

One of the most infamous residents was Justice of the Peace James "Jim" Burnett, who ran the town and was, in effect, a corrupt dictator of considerable power. He was murdered in Tombstone in 1897. You will read what some residents of Charleston thought of Burnett in this chapter.

Much like the upriver town of Fairbank, Charleston and Millville suffered a double whammy that crushed the communities as effectively as the mills crushed silver ore.

The mines in Tombstone flooded in 1886, forcing a shutdown at the mills. The reason for the towns' existence was wiped out. A large earthquake and a series of disastrous aftershocks in 1887 ruined every adobe structure in town.

By 1889 Charleston was a ghost town. The destruction of the town continued, often due to flooding of the San Pedro, which has swept away many of the original buildings and is encroaching on more. Additionally, the town was used for live-fire training during World War II by the Ninety-third Infantry Division stationed at Fort Huachuca in the nearby City of Sierra Vista. A careful observer can sometimes find adobe walls penetrated by nineteenth century rifle and revolver shells mixed in with the occasional twentieth century shell from a World War II era "tommy gun."

Although the businesses left and man and nature are reducing the community to little more than a footnote in the history books, many of those who lived and worked in Charleston decided to stick around. Some of them were willing to speak.

Access to Charleston and Millville is from a parking lot immediately east of Charleston Road. The trip to Millville is easy and follows a wide path. The way into Charleston follows a railroad bed abandoned in 2012 and requires crossing the San Pedro on foot. The crossing can be as easy as tip-toeing across a shallow stream. It can also be impossible. During the summer monsoon season the tip-toe area can be under more than seventeen feet of dark, raging water. The day we showed up we crossed on a log using sticks like ski poles to keep our balance.

Session One

D: This is EVP session one—Charleston. Dan, Rhonda, and Dwight at the place we call The Bar. It is approximately 10:08 a.m. on January 7, 2017. And we're going to do a quick EVP session here at the bar. (Microphone interference.) If you can hear me I'd really like you to come up and say something real loud to us so we can hear you.

DB: Setting down the recorder.

D: Well, this is a bar, so bartender if you're here I need a beer. Can you get me a beer?

DB: What's the special drink of the house? What do you recommend?

R: I take it he has a special?

DB: Everybody has a special.

R: Right, but it was circling…

DB: Right. They were big on mixed drinks. Like Dwight said, the whiskey was so bad.

R: Do you have a rum and coke?

DB: No. They don't know what a coke is.

D: You said coke and they don't have any idea.

R: Okay, do you have rum?

D: I'm getting a yes.

R: Okay. Mix that with whatever.

DB: He's saying no.

R: Okay, I'll have it straight, straight rum. Straight up. Do you have ice?

No.

DB: I'm getting a no.

R: I'll take my rum straight up then, a straight shot. Okay.

DB: Can you tell us your name please?

The pendulum said no.

R: Is there a Jack here?

DB: The pendulum said yes.

R: Is Jack the bartender? Or one of the bartenders?

DB: I'm getting a yes.

There are people in the background. (Tourists in the area.)

R: Yeah. I don't know where they are.

DB: Up on the railroad track.

Yes.

R: Do you look after this place?

DB: I'm getting a yes.

R: Are there more than five spirits here?

DB: A good solid yes.

R: Are there more than ten spirits here?

DB: Strong no.

R: Are there eight spirits here?

DB: I'm getting a yes.

D: Are there any ladies in the house with us today?

DB: Yes.

Are there any ladies *of* the house here with us today?

No. They're guests.

D: Ladies we certainly thank you for being here with us. Kind of a rough and tumble town for some ladies to be here, but we appreciate you being here.

Did you like it in Charleston when you were here?

R: Yes.

DB: I'm getting a yes.

R: Did you have children?

I should address … There are a lot of people.

Somebody said no.

DB: Is there more than one female here?

There are at least two.

R: Did one of you have a son about ten?

DB: Stomach noise. And that's a strong yes.

R: And did you have a dog, a real fluffy dog? Medium size?

DB: I'm getting a yes.

R: Remember we've seen a dog, a boy with a dog?

D: Yep.

Let me ask—is there anybody here that knows Justice Jim Burnett?

DB: I'm getting a yes over here.

D: Okay. We understand that Justice Jim ran this town. Is that true?

DB: I got a yes.

D: Let me ask—did you like Justice Jim Burnett?

DB: I'm getting a pretty strong no.

D: Yep.

DB: What are you getting?

R: No.

DB: Just for the record, nobody can see me do my pendulum work. My back is to Dwight and Rhonda, so we're not reading each other.

R: No. They hated him.

DB: I get a … wow. I get a strong yes on that.

D: Old Justice Jim was quite a figure here. We understand that. Was he ever in this building with you?

DB: I get a solid yes.

D: I imagine old Jim came into a lot of these buildings collecting taxes and shaking people down. Is that true?

DB: Strong yes over here.

R: Uh-hm.

(Rhonda coughs.)

DB: Different pollens.

R: Did he make any threats to you? This is for the ladies, did he make any threats, any improper threats?

DB: I'm getting a strong yes.

R: Yep.

DB: Care to comment on that, please?

R: Them or me?

DB: I'd like the ladies' perspective.

D: Can you tell us in just a few words, can you tell us what he may have said to you? (Pause.)

Well, okay. We thank you for talking with us today and communicating with us today. We're going to be in town for a while and you're welcome to stay with us or join us …

R: Yeah.

D: …or people you know who want to talk to us. We're not here to make fun of you or anything like that. We're just here to learn the history of this place. We love the history and we just like to talk to you folks and we appreciate the fact that you're nice enough to talk back to us. So, ladies and gentlemen you have a great day and we'll talk to you real soon.

DB: We appreciate it.

D: End of EVP session one.

DB: End session one.

Session Two—Rhonda recording on video

D: Okay, we are recording. EVP Session Two. We don't know what building this is. It's approximately…

DB: Ten thirty-five

D: …ten thirty-five on January 7, 2017. We're just going to do a quick pendulum session here. We're going to have the recorder as backup. Okay.

DB: Is there anyone here that's willing to speak?

I'm getting a yes.

What's your intuition picking up?

D: I'm getting that there's at least one person here. I'm getting that it's… is the person here female?

DB: That's a strong yes.

D: Yeah, that's what I'm picking up.

DB: I got goose bumps. That's … she wants to talk.

D: Yep. Was this your house?

DB: Strong yes.

D: Okay. We've come to your place several times. Did you, ma'am, if I can ask you, did you cook meals for the workers?

DB: I'm getting a yes.

D: I see her in that kind of a position where she …

DB: Yeah.

D: … feeds a lot of people.

DB: I'm getting strong answers.

D: So she's here. Ma'am, can you not so much for the pendulum, but can you tell us what your name is?

Okay, I got a really strong name here.

DB: What name did you get?

D: Ma'am, is your name Mary?

DB: You got it.

D: Yep. Mary, thank you so …

KNOCK

… much for talking to us today. We heard a big knock right behind us here.

DB: Was that you, Mary?

Look at that. (pendulum "yes" movement reference)

D: Wow.

DB: Thank you, Mary.

D: Thank you for letting us know you're here in a way that we can understand. It's a little hard to communicate, but we're doing our best.

DB: Look at that.

D: That's a heck of a swing.

DB: I think we have a strong woman in the community.

D: Yeah.

DB: Well, you had to be.

D: You had to be to do what she did.

Did you see a lot of... Let me try to rephrase the question for you, Mary. It's kind of hard right now, but, you saw a lot of comings and goings in town here, did you?

(Unidentified sound.)

Okay, Mary, I just picked up something. I think you're trying to tell me something here. Mary, did you lose your husband here?

DB: I'm getting a yes.

D: Okay. I'm picking up that … Mary, did your husband die in an accident?

DB: It started going yes the second you said "ac … "

D: Okay, that's what I'm getting. Mary, I'm sorry about that. It kind of left you in a position, didn't it?

DB: Umm … yes.

D: Mary is when your husband passed, is that when you kind of took over basically caretaker of the camp and started cooking for folks?

DB: Yes.

D: It kind of gave you a purpose, didn't it?

(Gunfire in background: Hunters were in the area— volume of gunshot noise extremely low.)

DB: That's gunfire.

D: Yeah, that's gunfire in the back. Yep.

DB: She said yes. Well, she would know.

D: Yes. She would certainly know. Well, Mary, we're going to be here a while. I really want to thank you for talking with us and communicating with us. Before we go ahead and stop what we're doing here, is there something you would like to tell us?

DB: She's telling me yes.

D: Yep.

DB: Speak up, please.

D: Yeah. Yeah. I've got this little box in my hand, Mary, if you talk really loud next to it or next to us we'll probably be able to hear you on this. If you can do that for us…

Okay. Thank you, Mary. One more question before we stop. Would you like us to come back sometime and visit with you?

DB: That's a big, strong yes.

D: Okay.

DB: I think she likes company.

D: And, well, she's used to having it around her all the time with the people… Okay, Mary, I can give you our solid promise we will come back and we will talk to you and visit you and I want to thank you so much for talking with us today. And we will be back, Mary. Thank you.

KNOCK

DB: Thank you very much. That wasn't a gunshot.

D: No. I'm going to…

DB: Get a close-up of the pendulum. (Dwight shot video of pendulum movement.)

R: Yeah.

DB: Just a real tight close up.

R: Yeah.

DB: Fifteen seconds.

Okay. I think she was a strong-willed woman.

R: I didn't know if that was a water bottle in my thing, but … (reference to sound)

The multiple knocking sounds heard during this session were not from hunters' gunfire. Both sounds can be heard on the recording and they are distinctive. The knocks, whatever they represent, came from within the adobe structure.

DB: I am recording.

DB: EVP Session Two for me. For Dan three.

We're at, for lack of a better term, "Dwight's Hole." It's a square hole in the ground that we found that we think is a well. Again, this is January 7, 2017 at approximately time of …

DB: Eleven oh-seven.

D: Eleven oh-seven. I'm going to … We're going to try to recreate a little bit of a former EVP session that we did so I'm going to put my recorder down on the very same rock.

DB: My recorder is down in the grass next to the well.

D: Hands free.

DB: Hands free.

D: I am in … I am standing in the hole just for reference. Is there anybody here with us right now that would like to talk to us or communicate with us?

(Camera noise.)

R: That was my camera.

DB: The pendulum is swinging yes.

R: Do you want me to record this with your camera.

DB: That's okay. It's kind of weedy.

D: We had a tough time again finding this little slice of heaven and we'd really like to know how we can easily find this place and how to mark this area. Can you tell us how to mark this area, please?

For recording purposes there is a bird kind of yelling in the background there.

I think we already established that there's somebody here.

DB: I got a yes.

D: Okay, let's go with more of a pendulum thing, then. Is the person who is here with us, are you a male?

DB: I'm getting a yes.

D: Sir, if you're willing to, can you tell us what your name is?

R: Does it begin with the letter B? Do either of your names begin with a B?

DB: I got a pretty strong yes on that one.

D: Okay, sir, do you … this may seem like a pretty stupid question. Sir, do you carry a gun, a pistol?

DB: I got a yes, a weak yes, but a yes.

D: Okay. Okay, sir, I don't even know where I'm going with that.

R: Have you fired your pistol lately?

DB: I'm getting a yes.

R: Let me ask you this: have you ever shot somebody?

DB: I got an immediate no.

D: Okay, for the man who is here, the hole I'm standing in, was this a well?

DB: I am getting a no.

D: Was this like a storage, cold storage?

DB: I am getting a yes.

D: Okay, and just so we cover all the bases, was this area, was this hole ever used as a … I'll say a bathroom, an outhouse?

DB: That's a pretty good no.

D: Okay, I just wanted to hit all the possibilities and get answers on all of them. Okay, so we're pretty well established that this was cold storage. Was this cold storage for beer and liquor?

DB: Strong yes.

D: Okay. So, was the building in front of me, was this a hotel?

DB: No. I got a no.

D: Was it a restaurant?

DB: For that I'm getting a yes.

D: I guess maybe you didn't call them restaurants back in the day. Was it like an eating place or boarding house?

DB: For me you have to ask one or the other.

D: Okay. Was this building a boarding house?

DB: That is a no.

D: Was this place more of an eatery, a place where you can eat.

DB: I'm getting a yes.

R: Or drink, obviously.

D: I sure thank you for that, for clearing that up for us because we weren't really sure.

DB: I don't know where this is coming from, but is the number three significant, for some reason?

I got a yes. I don't know where that came from.

D: The number three…

DB: The number three. And is the number three significant to the individual here?

No.

Is it significant to the place?

Yes.

Again, I don't know where that came from.

D: For recording purposes, in case we're picking it up, there are voices far away from us like kids yelling.

R: And gunshots.

DB: Hunters.

D: So we do have kids in the area.

So the number three to this area, is that right?

DB: To the place, yeah. Not a person, but to the place. Maybe that was Bar #3 or something. I have no idea. Maybe your intuition picks up something.

R: I'm going to go live, but only on you. I'm not going to show Dan. (Facebook reference.)

DB: (joking) Ah!

R: Well, I didn't know if you wanted me to shoot, to show the pendulum.

DB: (joking) It's okay. It's all right. I'm not in it for fame and fortune like *some* people.

R: If you want to post. Do you mind if I go live with you?

DB: No. I don't mind. Just tell me to hold my stomach in.

R: I'm getting ready to push the button. I don't know how long it will last.

DB: Again, I'm getting strong, strong pendulum swings here so there's lots of activity here.

D: So we got the number three.

(R narrating FB live in background.)

D: And we got the number three that's connected to this area, so let me ask you this: We've already established that the building next to us was kind of an eatery. Did the name of the eatery have to do with the number three?

DB: That's a real strong yes.

D: Okay. So, was more like the "Three something" or the "something Three"?

DB: Yeah.

D: We will definitely research that.

DB: I'm thinking Bar #3 or the Three Brothers' Saloon...

D: Or three peaks... that's kind of what I'm picking up.

R: Just for recording purposes, I just whispered. I forgot the number one...

D: You were... it [cellphone] disconnected there for a while.

R: Sorry about the connection. I don't know if it's spirits. Let's see.

D: Clearly we're in a …

R: Yeah, there are a lot of trees here, so I don't know if it's going to last.

DB: This is strong. There is a lot of activity here, strong activity.

D: To the male that is here that we are talking to now, was this a busy area when you were here?

DB: Again, yes.

D: Okay. Did you live close to here and by close I mean … did you live close to here?

DB: Yeah.

Ask him if he knew Mary.

D: Oh, yeah. We just came from a house where we talked to a female named Mary who did a lot of cooking for the workers. Did you know Mary?

DB: Big, strong yes.

D: Well, they're in the same sort of business, I guess.

Did you work at the eatery here?

DB: That's a no.

D: Did you eat at this building.

DB: That's a good, strong yes.

D: Okay. Let me ask you this: did you eat over at Mary's house? Did she cook you stuff?

DB: Big, strong yes.

D: So they knew each other.

R: Were you married to Mary?

DB: No. I got a no.

D: Well, that's … we got some answers anyway. Sir, I'd like to thank you for talking to us and taking the time with us today. We're just really interested in your history and why you're here and what you did while you were here. We're going to be in town a little while longer so if you'd care to follow us around and talk with us, that's fine. We're going to go ahead and wrap it up for our little session here, but thank you so much for being here with us.

If you can tell us one more time how we can find this place easier the next time we come that would be great.

Okay. Thank you so much.

DB: We appreciate it.

I'm picking up the recorder and session over.

We sat down later for a fourth session. As previously noted, hunters and kids were in the area and at times we clearly heard shouting. Dwight and Rhonda's intuitive abilities indicated that perhaps someone else had joined in the shouting. As you will see this proved to be true.

DB: Okay, recording.

D: Okay. We are in the Charleston ghost town in a place we call the Glass Field, which is right behind several buildings. And to drive home the point one more time, it is January 7, 2017 at approximately noonish—one o'clock.

DB: Right at noon.

D: Right at noon. Okay.

So we're just going to do a quick session just to see if anybody is hanging around their old junk. If there is somebody here with us…

DB: Recorder down.

D: Okay, you can … well, let me ask this: is there somebody here with us now?

DB: Yeah.

D: Okay.

DB: I got a yes.

D: Did you live in one of these buildings behind us.

DB: That's a pretty strong yes.

D: Strong yes. Did you also work in one of these buildings behind us?

DB: Continuing yes.

D: Okay.

DB: Let Rhonda ask a question or two.

R: Are you ... did you just shout a few minutes ago?

DB: That's a yes with a kick.

R: Are you from the South?

DB: That's a no.

R: Okay, are you from the East Coast?

DB: That's a yes.

R: Are you from ... I don't know ... somewhere where they have a bit of an accent.

D: Boston or ...

DB: Bahs-ton.

R: ... Or Virginia.

DB: Well, pick one.

R: Massachusetts?

DB: No.

R: Virginia?

DB: Virginia—I got a yes.

D: Okay.

DB: That works.

That's enough video.

D: That's fine.

R: Did you … oh, sorry.

DB: Go ahead, since we're doing a session.

D: Yeah.

DB: Rock 'n roll.

R: Did you know any of the Clantons?

DB: Oh, yeah. Strong yes.

R: Are you a Clanton?

DB: No.

DB: Did you like the Clantons?

That's a pretty good yes.

D: Yep.

R: And you are a male? Is that right?

DB: Did you like the Earp faction?

That kicked no real fast.

D: That stopped and kicked a no real quick.

DB: No wasted time on that.

D: Sorry, but we had to ask.

Did you ever eat at Ike's lunch counter?

DB: That's another yes.

R: Did you work in Millville?

DB: No. That's a no.

R: So you worked here in Charleston? Okay.

DB: That's another yes.

R: (Stomach noise.) That's my stomach I think.

D: Okay. We'll probably wrap it up from here.

DB: I've got what I need. I just want to give him some stuff to work with. (Reference to images for a video project.)

R: Thank you for talking to us.

DB: We appreciate it.

D: Absolutely.

R: If you can talk really loud into this little black box … anything else you want to say, we can pick up your voice.

DB: Just speak into this box if you would. Just say anything. Say your name.

D: Yep. Just shout it out.

Okay.

DB: End of session.

D: Thank you.

The EVPs

One of the most remarkable EVP recordings in this book was captured by Dwight and Rhonda at an earlier visit to

Charleston, specifically at the place we referred to as Dwight's Hole. They had just discovered the site and were wondering how to mark it when a gunshot rang out. Although clearly recorded, neither Dwight nor Rhonda heard the gunshot until they played back the audio.

R: I think we need to, like, mark the tree with …

D: Something.

R: … something. I don't know with what.

EVP: (Gunshot) … with bloodshed …

To listen to the EVPs go to:

www.beelieveparanormal.com/our-book.html

10

That's *John* Ringo

John Ringo, popularly known as Johnny Ringo or just Ringo, died and is buried in a lone grave in southeastern Arizona. Dwight approaches the gravesite with the same sense of history, awe, and respect that I feel walking through the plaza where another John (Kennedy) was murdered. There are very few parallels between the Dealey Plaza and Turkey Creek incidents: JFK was a popularly elected president; John Ringo was a self-made alcoholic. But each is an historic figure, a murder victim destined to live on in fact and legend long after most of us cross over to whatever fate or choice awaits us. Someone doesn't have to be psychic to feel a sense of being in the presence of history in such places, whether surrounded by the skyscrapers of Dallas or the tall pines of the Chiricahua Mountains. What really happened to John Ringo here is a matter of much speculation—for some.

*Dan, Dwight, and Rhonda outside of
the fence near John Ringo's gravesite.*

*Dan and Rhonda combine pendulum dowsing
and intuitive skills to communicate with John Ringo.*

And why should we refer to Ringo as *John* and not *Johnny* as he is portrayed in film, television, radio, and print?

Because he said so.

A Fast Verdict at West Turkey Creek

As with many Wild West characters, their history is a careening mix of fact, fiction, and folly. That rule certainly applies to the mysterious death of the man now known just as Ringo, one of the most famous and iconic names in all of Western history. He has been portrayed in popular media as hero, anti-hero, villain, and victim. The truth is probably lost somewhere in those conflicting tales.

John Peters Ringo (sometimes spelled Ringgold) rode into Arizona Territory in 1879 and eventually took up with the infamous cowboy element in and around Tombstone. The cowboys were rustlers, thieves, and murderers, and so threatened the peace that the President of the United States threatened marshal law. Their raiding into Mexico was so intense that at one time the government feared war was inevitable unless the gang was corralled. But many of the cowboys were also legitimate businessmen. Ike Clanton owned a restaurant and several ranches. Other members of the gang were ranchers, saloon owners, and businessmen. As in much of Western history, who you were depended largely on your attitude, who you met on the street, or in the saloon, the time of day, or the amount of "tangleleg" you had consumed. Ringo consumed a lot of "tangleleg" and was known to have a bad temper when drunk.

He often threw verbal punches at Doc Holliday and was an enemy of Wyatt Earp and his brothers. It is suspected, but has never been proved, that Ringo participated in the wounding of Virgil Earp and the murder of Morgan Earp. In a "well, that's Arizona for you" episode, Wyatt Earp set out leading a *federal* posse to track down the killers (the famous vendetta ride). Cochise County Sheriff Johnny Behan then organized a *state* posse to track down the federal posse. Ringo was one of the nineteen members of that party, but the two groups never crossed paths.

In July 1882 Ringo went on a drunken binge. On July 14th a teamster traveling from West Turkey Creek found his body sitting in the fork of a nearby oak tree with a bullet hole in the top left side of his head. July in Arizona is hot and deceased persons exposed to the elements did not hold up well under such conditions. A coroner's jury was called on the spot and it was determined that Ringo had committed suicide. He had a bullet hole in his temple, the bullet exiting through the back of his head. He was buried on the spot.

The suicide verdict isn't accepted by all. His feet were wrapped in pieces of his undershirt. His revolver was hanging by one finger. A small portion of his forehead and part of his hair had been removed, apparently by a knife. The belt for his revolver cartridges was buckled on upside-down. Curiously for a victim of a shot through the skull, his hat was still on his head. Two weeks later his horse was found. Ringo's boots were still tied to the saddle.

Many authors say it was murder. Suspects include Wyatt Earp, Doc Holliday, "Buckskin" Frank Leslie, and Michael O'Rourke (Johnny Behind-the-Duce). In the hopes of adding some legitimate information to the historical record, we decided to go to the source.

Heating Up a Cold Case

John Ringo was one of Dwight's favorite characters in the West. "I was always interested in the West and John Ringo just fascinated me—his persona and the stories about him," Dwight said. His interest was heightened when he and Rhonda moved to Sierra Vista, Arizona and met one of their new neighbors. Kandace (Kandie) Sanders was surprisingly familiar with the case because her family owned the ranch where Ringo was killed. She offered to take them to the site; an offer they immediately accepted.

They were able to meet her uncle who lived there all his life. The Sanders family lived on that property for generations, so the stories told were as firsthand as possible, handed down from the people who lived there during the times in question. "The best way to describe it is to say that it was my Graceland," said Dwight. "Just walking out there experiencing that feeling and that energy on that hallowed ground and basically knowing that this is where it happened. This is where one of my Western heroes still is. He's buried there. It was just a very in-your-gut, spiritual experience out there."

In talking with the family they learned that the death—ruled a suicide at the time—was still carried as an open case in Cochise County. The family's side of the story brought up a number of serious questions. "I heard a completely different story than what is told in the papers and that really got me thinking and researching it after that," said Dwight. "You could see both sides—either murder or suicide—and the more I looked into the suicide, it just didn't make any sense, forensically or any other way."

The couple was committed to bringing the case out of a dark past and into the light of modern investigation. The first step was to do a lot of research in the archives to find out anything they could regarding the death, beginning with the coroner's report and some eyewitness testimony from people who were around there at the time and who wrote reports of the incident.

The big moment came during a psychic investigation and an EVP session and actually hearing answers to their questions, Dwight said, "That made me think, 'Now wait a minute…he's saying something different from what appeared in the papers.' I asked him, 'Did you commit suicide?' I got a no. This was from John Ringo on the recorder. So, the quest began."

He and Rhonda put together a really solid package about their investigation and then contacted the Cochise

County Sheriff's Office through Sheriff Mark Daniels. They told him that the case should be at least reopened to "undetermined" as far as cause of death. Rhonda commented, "We weren't trying to pin a murderer at this point. We just wanted them to reevaluate it." They had several conversations with Daniels. The response, not unexpected, was that the county just didn't have the financial and manpower resources to reopen such an old case.

Dwight said, "He did look over all our stuff and said that it was extremely interesting and that it was thought provoking."

As of this writing the case is in a stalemate. Daniels is interested in the case, but again the bureaucracy and red tape have blocked progress for the moment. "We have thought about contacting different pathologists to see if they would be interested in looking over our stuff because they have the power to reopen a case as well. They haven't given up and are always looking for new avenues of approach. If we have a pathologist who sees something that could possibly change it, then they legally have the power to open it to at least undetermined status," Dwight said. "We've not gone that route, but it may be a way to go."

Meeting John Ringo

One of the first things Dwight and Rhonda discovered about Ringo was that he did not like to be called Johnny. Dwight said, "My first time out there I was doing an EVP session and I walked up there and said, 'Johnny Ringo. Okay,

Johnny, we're here for you. We want to hear your story.' As soon as I was done saying that we got a really gruff EVP saying, 'Fuck the Johnny.' At that point I was like, okay, so it's John or Mr. Ringo from here on out. I'm absolutely convinced that the voice recorded is the voice of John Ringo. I respect his wishes."

Again, our approach on every investigation was non-confrontational. We sought positive interaction, not conflict, with any spirit willing to invest time with us. This approach has led to an increase in the knowledge base about spirits, the spirit world, and the afterlife "over there."

Obviously, the top question on their minds concerned the nature of Ringo's death. Was it truly a suicide or was it murder? The trip was conducted as an investigation of a crime scene. Dwight said, "Measuring the distance across the wash, Kelsie Sanders (ranch owner's descendent) asked Ringo point-blank if Frank Leslie was the one who murdered him. We got a yes. Now whether that voice is John Ringo or whomever, we did get a yes, a very faint and light yes, but a very definite yes." The voice was identical to the voice they captured on other EVPs at the site.

It's impossible to say for sure, but Dwight and Rhonda believe they spoke directly to the spirit of John Ringo.

People who have looked at the evidence and who have taken the time to visit the site believe the killer was Frank Leslie because he was seen in the area and had asked if anyone had seen John Ringo. He asked Mr. Sanders, who was a teamster at the ranch at that time.

Additional investigations revealed the presence of other spirits out there. One of them was an older man or someone who sounded like an older man on the EVPs. A male friend accompanied Dwight to the site hoping to capture more EVPs. Dwight took his usual polite and respectful approach, but his friend became confrontational. He called Ringo a back shooter among other things. This continued until he finished the tirade and said, "Now what do you think about that?"

An older man's voice (recorded) said, "Oh, no. Don't say that."

It was very clear and it was not the same voice that they had recorded before. Further research into the Sanders Ranch history turned up the fact that one of the relatives who lived on the ranch around that time was thrown from his horse and crushed by a wagon right there at the ranch house, so there was a tragic death in the family there as well. "I'm thinking it was that person as the second voice, someone who is staying around and watching over his ranch," Dwight said.

On another trip they encountered a child, a girl that has not been identified. She was calling out, "Mommy, mommy, come help me" in a clear, child's voice.

"It was one of those times during an investigation that just breaks your heart," Rhonda said, "because you hear a child in need, a small child, and of course we didn't listen to this until we got home and we were like, 'Aghh.' We have somebody out there who really needs help and we didn't hear it at the time and now we have to go back out and try to talk to her and try to help her." That story is yet to be concluded.

Historical research is essential (whenever possible) in paranormal research. For example, as with the gravesite of Mattie Earp, the actual burial place of John Peters Ringo isn't the official plot seen by the tourists who drop by. If someone is visiting such a site it is only polite and respect-ful to attempt communication at the actual location. It's impossible to say, but considering Ringo's temperament, it is possible that he would resent an investigator paying attention to a false location for his grave. Accuracy is not only important in conducting this type of work; it is also a sign of respect for those who have crossed over.

Ringo at Rest at Last

We arrived at the gravesite in June of 2016. Dwight and Rhonda had been to the location many times before. The gravesite is on private property, but is marked, easily acces-sible, and open to the public. A wide, "washboard" dirt road leads to a barbed-wire fence with a metal gate. A narrow pathway leads through tall grass and scattered pine and juniper trees to the edge of a cattle tank—an area that over-looks West Turkey Creek some 100 yards away. The ranch house of Ringo's friend Will Sanders was and still is about

50 yards distant. The official gravesite is marked by a large pile of stones with a painted rock headstone. "John Ringo July 13, 1882" is inscribed in dark letters on white paint. An Arizona state plaque is nearby. "John Ringo—The remains of this noted gunman and outlaw lie here."

The actual site of John Ringo's grave is nearby, but it is unmarked and will not be further identified here.

Rhonda sensed spirit activity from the moment she stepped through the gate. "Absolutely. I knew there were people there … spirits there. And I knew John was there. That's why when we were walking up the pathway I told them that we were coming up there to talk."

We walked easily to the actual gravesite and stood around a moment to get acclimated to it and to let the impact of history sink in. "This is an interesting, hallowed place," Dwight said, "at least for me anyway. Even when I was a kid I heard the name John Ringo and heard the stories about the gunfight at the OK Corral and all the characters in Tombstone. I've always been a big fan of John Ringo."

While getting ready to conduct an EVP session, Dwight revealed his theory of how John Ringo died. "Buckskin" Frank Leslie and Billy Claiborne were the killers. They traveled up through Turkey Creek close to sunset and came up out of the creek about 100 to 125 yards east/northeast of where Ringo was camped on a bluff. They were hidden and well-protected by trees, brush, and other vegetation on the flats. "That's where I think Buckskin saw his shot, so to speak. He took his rifle out, knelt down, and shot Ringo once in the head." Dwight conducted a forensic examination of the area at the site and down on the flats. "We took GPS coordinates of the area where I feel Buckskin was. I did that by looking at the open terrain, looking at the open areas, and determined where I would be if I had to take a shot at somebody. So I plotted that point, plotted where the tree was, basically, and figured in a five-foot-eight, five-foot-ten-inch man and plotted those GPS coordinates, and it wasn't until after we got home that I got everything into the computer and got a look at everything. The angle of a rifle shot from that point would have matched the angle in John's head from the right temple to the outside to the left, coming out. That was kinda' the telling of the tale there."

Billy Claiborne, who had run from the gunfight at the OK Corral, was brought down in another gunfight outside the Oriental Saloon in Tombstone. "Buckskin" Frank Leslie was the man who pulled the trigger. The killing was ruled justifiable homicide, but some speculate that the killing was related to Claiborne's knowledge of the Ringo killing.

We conducted a 15-minute session right next to the gravesite, but did not get any clear EVPs. Apparently five to six spirits, including John Ringo, were present. The combination of intuition and pendulum dowsing did produce some interesting results. I said at the time, "It's surprising to me considering this is where he was murdered, but all three of us got the definite impression that he is perfectly happy being right where he is."

Rhonda said, "Absolutely. He's hanging out with the Sanderses and anybody else who's there. It's a very pretty, happy place. It's not a place where you feel a need to help somebody cross over. They don't want to cross over. It's not a place where anybody would be *stuck*."

In earlier visits to the sight, Dwight and Rhonda did capture some startling EVPs.

The EVPs

D: I believe we've solved this one.

EVP: Oh, don't say it.

D: Because this is the inside of the tree here.

Sources for additional reading on John Ringo include:

John Ringo: The Gunfighter Who Never Was

Inventing Wyatt Earp by Allen Barra

Doc Holiday by Gary L. Roberts

To listen to the EVPs go to:

www.beelieveparanormal.com/our-book.html

Wyatt Earp: The Life Behind the Legend by Casey Tefertiller

The best research material on the Earp years in Tombstone is *A Tenderfoot in Tombstone: The Private Journal of George Whitwell Parsons.*

11

An Angel at the Jail Tree

Native Americans mined turquoise in the southeastern end of Arizona's Dragoon Mountains for countless years, so it was natural for the Anglos who first settled here to name their town after that semiprecious blue stone. Tiffany & Company purchased the mines and the name Turquoise was set in place above the post office door. The town under that name lasted from 1890–1894. The name was changed in 1900 after John Gleeson began mining operations nearby. More than the name was changed. The entire town moved closer to Gleeson's holdings. In the boom and bust era of the Old West it was common practice for towns to move lock, stock, barrel, roof, and wall from a bust to the latest boomtown.

Dan is standing outside of the Gleeson jail building.

Dwight and Dan communicating with spirits at Gleeson ghost town.

Dwight examines the chain from the town's infamous "jail tree."

The people of Gleeson suffered a number of fires. The big fire in 1912 burned twenty-eight buildings. The townspeople rebuilt, but by then the community had been burnt out in more ways than one and it never really recovered. Today many ruins mark the location, including the remains of a school, the Silver Saloon, "Kitty House" Yee Wee's Chinese Restaurant, a variety store, and a jail.

Before the jail was built, the citizens used a standard Old West method of securing troublemakers—the "Jail Tree." This was fairly common in the Old West. As towns sprang up almost overnight, construction of a true jail was at the end of the priority list and well behind mining structures, saloons, cafes, general stores and bordellos. Often a tree in or near town served the purpose until folks got around to building a formal structure.

We had led a group of people to Gleeson as part of Dwight and Rhonda's "A Haunting in the Desert" fundraiser for the Wounded Warriors organization. A return trip for some one-on-one (we hoped) paranormal communication seemed in order. The old jail has been restored and is now a museum. After a pleasant conversation with the museum caretaker, Bob, we began in the warm sunlight outside, near an old jail door on display in the porch area.

September 17, 2016

D: We are sitting outside the front doors of the jail, ironically near the original jail door, and we're going to do an EVP-slash-pendulum session and then after that I want to do just a real quick EVP session without the pendulum to see if we can differentiate between the two. I'll set the recorder down on the bench. Hands free.

We'll just start out by doing a quick welcome here and, you know, if there is somebody here, we really appreciate that you're here with us and allowing us to be here with you. This is your home or your spot, not ours. We're just visitors, so I want to thank you for that. I guess let me start out generally here. Is there somebody here with us now?

R: Yes.

DB: I was getting a strong yes … I was getting a strong reading on the pendulum that there is someone here.

D: Okay. Is the person here someone in the law enforcement field?

DB: I am getting a no.

D: Okay.

DB: What are you getting, Rhonda?

R: No.

D: That's good. That's …

DB: I'm getting a strong no. The movement is real strong today.

D: That's good. We thank you for being here. I know you can't move or influence the pendulum for this question, but can you just come close and tell us what your name is because these two boxes will hear that and we'll be able to hear it later. If you could just come up close and state real loud what your name is that'd be great.

Okay. Thank you. We're also doing this pendulum … Dan's doing his pendulum here so you can, you know, use that. We're going to try to use yes or no questions. Is the person here with us … are you male?

D: I am getting a yes.

R: I'm getting a yes, too.

D: Were you a guest at this little gray bar hotel?

DB: I'm getting a no. (To Rhonda) What are you getting?

R: I'm getting a no. Do you want me to tell you what I'm getting or will that influence—

DB: No. Go ahead.

R: I'm getting that he lived on this land and before ... and he knew the land and he's watching out for the jail.

DB: Ask that question.

R: Do you ... did you have land out here?

DB: See I'm getting ... I'm getting an immediate yes.

R: Do you kinda' stay around here or are you here today looking after the jail, protecting it? Watching over it?

DB: I'm getting a null answer.

R: Is your last name Bono? (Question based on a conversation with the museum caretaker.)

DB: Well, that's a yes.

R: Okay. Do you watch over several properties out here? Over the land?

DB: That was a yes.

R: Is your name Joe?

DB: I got a yes. Let's do that again, just to be sure.

R: Okay. Is your name Joe Bono?

DB: Yes. (coughs.)

R: Do you need a cough drop, Dan? I have one.

DB: Unless that's Joe tickling my throat.

R: Joe, do you know who Bob is seeing up by the mines? Do you know who that is? (Reference is to a ghost seen at one of the mines.)

DB: Yes.

D: Is it you up by the mines?

DB: No.

D: I just wanted to clarify that.

R: Is it family?

DB: You'll need to …

R: Is it a female up there by the mines?

DB: That's sort of a hell no.

D: Wow.

DB: Real strong.

R: Is the person wearing a long coat?

DB: Yes. Is the person wearing a duster by any chance?

(A duster is a long coat worn outdoors to protect the wearer and his other clothing from dust much like a raincoat is used during a rainstorm.)

I'm getting a yes. That would explain the flowing.

R: Right.

D: It would, but it sure as hell wouldn't be a miner. A miner wouldn't be around a mine in a duster.

R: Is that person looking for somebody up there? Do you know?

DB: Yes. It could be a guard or just somebody looking around. It wouldn't have to be a miner.

D: Well, there were a lot of cowboys who came through this area and of course they are not miners.

DB: It could have been a miner in a rainstorm. Is the entity we're talking about up there wearing a duster?

Immediate yes.

Are you getting a different feeling? Or is that just logic intruding its ugly little head?

R: Do you know if this person who is male up there is looking for something they hid?

DB: I'm getting a no.

R: Do you know if they're looking for someone who died up there?

DB: That's a yes.

R: Okay.

D: Just for recording purposes we do have a couple of flies here that are flying around and could sound like voices on the recorder, so I just want to point that out.

R: So, I wonder if this person hasn't found his brother or whatever or whoever in the afterlife. That's just my…

DB: I got a yes. Ask that in a more direct way.

R: Is this person who is looking are they looking for a family member who they haven't been able to find?

Okay. That was my initial instinct.

D: Right.

R: Oh, God. I have a feeling that it's going to get emotional if we get over there. To me it sounds like he's frantically looking for…

DB: Yes.

R: … like a brother.

KNOCKS

R: Are you with your brother, Joe? Is your brother over there with you and your wife?

No?

Okay. He's probably with others.

DB: Is the brother a blood relation?

Yeah.

KNOCKS

R: So, are these your family members up by the mine?

DB: That's a yes.

R: Oh, my gosh.

D: Well, the Bonos have been here forever.

R: Do you think I'll be able to talk to your son and get more information. Okay.

DB: Again, yes.

R: I will do that. I will contact your son and see if he can tell me who might have passed up there and who the other person might be.

DB: Is it okay if we do that?

Yeah.

D: Okay.

R: Bob was so great telling us stories. Bob is a great guy. Telling us stories about the past and what went on and ...

DB: Good swing yes. Is that your stomach gurgling?

D: Yeah.

DB: Want to try it without the pendulum? Just to see what you get?

D: Yeah, let's close this down.

R: Thanks, Joe.

We moved across the road and down to the old Jail Tree, which still has metal cable wrapped around it. We stood in the shade and began our session.

D: EVP session four. We are now at the jail tree.

DB: Mine (recorder) is actually in the tree.

R: I think three or four men just joined us. Just letting you know.

D: There's been quite a bit of activity around here this morning. I don't know why. Now, this is pretty much a good representation of the book title *Time Served*.

R: Yep.

D: Can you imagine serving your time out here … chained to a tree.

DB: In a monsoon.

D: In a monsoon.

R: Oh, my God.

D: It's cool and wet during the night and 110 during the day.

DB: And humid.

D: This wasn't as big back then so I imagine it didn't provide as much shade.

R: Wind's blowing.

D: I cannot shake this little person who's here.

R: I just heard a child.

D: I ... there's been a little person ... I saw the little person when we were up there talking to those people. I took a couple of photos down this way.

R: I think it's a little girl.

D: I don't know.

DB: You guys are the intuitives so you know more than me.

R: I don't know why she's here. Maybe she was at the hospital.

D: I don't know.

DB: Maybe somebody she knew or was related to was chained to the tree.

D: Well, I get the feeling that she used to visit the people who were here.

DB: Kind of like a little ...

D: Candy Striper.

DB: Yeah.

D: Basically. I don't know if she brought 'em food.

R: Yeah, that could be.

D: I mean there's almost a sense of duty with this person. Not in an official sense.

R: In just a community sense.

D: Or moral obligation sense. Like this is where he or she came after school or wherever the school was at that time.

R: I think it was right beside it. The old school.

D: I don't know.

DB: It might have just been somebody with a good heart.

D: Some chatting up the hill. Well, you never know.

Ending my session. This is number five for me.

Dwight and Rhonda felt strongly that the little girl's spirit was leading us to the hospital. That became our next location. We arrived, looked around and settled for recording in a corner of the building out of the wind. Each of us felt that the location was a "hot" spot for paranormal contact.

DB: I'm setting it (recorder) down next to the wall.

D: EVP session six. I am now recording as well. We are at the southeast corner of the hospital.

DB: 11:20 (a.m.)

(To Rhonda) Tell somebody when you're going to take a picture so he can hold his stomach in.

I'm getting that there are multiple spirits here.

R: Yep. They're here.

DB: And that at least one is willing to communicate. Maybe they'll speak.

D: One is all we need.

R: That's generally how it works. You need a leader, a speaker for the group.

You want to ask the questions, Dwight?

D: You can. You're getting a pretty good response over there.

DB: They say the bugs are bothering them, too.

(Lots of mosquitos in the area)

I asked the question and got a very strong yes.

R: Nasty today.

D: That would have to have been an issue back then, I'd think.

DB: This was back before they (doctors) had anything to do with malaria … except suffer.

R: Is there … so we know that there are spirits here. Are there more than ten spirits here?

DB: I'm getting a yes.

R: Are there more than twenty, not including us?

DB: I'm getting a no.

R: Are there more than 15?

DB: Yes.

R: Did you have to count?

DB: No.

R: Well, thank you for talking with us today. Is the person who is coming forward female? Are you a woman?

DB: Yep.

R: Did you work here in the hospital?

DB: I'm getting a no.

R: Were you a patient?

DB: Yes.

R: Did you pass here at the hospital? Did you cross over? Did you die at the hospital?

DB: It kicked up yes when you said die.

R: Was it from disease?

DB: I'm getting a yes.

R: Thank you.

You want to ask some questions, Dwight?

DB: You can ask questions, open-ended questions, and I can try to verify whether that is right or wrong.

R: Okay.

DB: We don't purely have to stick with yes or no if something else comes to mind.

D: I'm just trying to hone in on anything right now.

R: Did your name start with an M?

DB: That's a yes.

R: I'm getting that. It's the name of one of my great, great grandparents.

DB: I wonder if you're here because you want to be here. That's a yes.

R: Does anybody in the group need help?

DB: Rephrase. I'm getting a null.

I got a null, Hull.

R: Are you all here of your own free will? Are you all just visiting here?

DB: Make it more individual.

R: Okay.

DB: Is there someone or …

R: Okay. Is there someone among the group that is here with you who needs help?

DB: Okay, that's a yes.

R: Have they not crossed over, so to speak?

DB: Yep. Let me ask something. Is there more than one entity in that specific situation?

Yeah. Several people.

R: Dwight, do you want to …

D: You're doing all right.

R: Are you here to help them move on?

DB: That's a real strong yes.

R: Is that why everybody is here to help—

DB: Whoa! Strong yes.

R: Okay. Is there a specific reason why the people who need help aren't moving on?

DB: Yes.

R: Did they commit crimes? No.

DB: I asked mentally and got a yes on "fear."

D: This wasn't really a rough-and-tumble place.

R: No, it wasn't, but you never know who came through here or what their reason might be.

DB: I'm getting a yes on this wasn't a rough-and-tumble place. Not like downtown Tombstone. Working people.

D: Working people. Country folks, so to speak, and not really citified.

R: Are they all adults?

DB: (quickly) No!

R: So there are children among the group who need help?

DB: Yes.

More than one?

No. So there's one child here.

R: Was the little girl that we saw by the tree the one who needs...

DB: That's a yes.

That's the little girl you saw?

She's scared to cross over.

R: Is she with family here?

DB: No, she is not.

Is that what you're getting?

R: Yes.

DB: We're on the same beam.

Is she afraid of what might happen to her on the other side?

No.

R: Is she afraid she won't be able to find her parents, her family?

To the little girl who is here, just go with this lady. She will help you. She'll help you find your parents and your family. It's okay. You don't have to be afraid. I think the whole group will help you and protect you.

DB: Confirmation on that.

Is the little girl attached to somebody here?

I'm getting a yes on that. I'm getting a feeling that she is afraid to leave someone here more so than she's afraid of what's waiting on the other side.

D: That could easily be.

R: Here as in dead here or living here?

DB: Ask a couple of different ways, but I'm getting a yes on spirit.

She might be the caretaker.

R: Well, I think she was over there (referring to jail tree). But they all need to go. They all need to … but you can come back to visit, obviously because that's how some of the people are here. They're visiting, so just because you go over there and find your parents and your family doesn't mean you can't come back and visit if you want. You need to be reunited with your family and you need to take everybody else with you. Can you do that?

DB: I'm getting a yes.

I asked if she's willing to cross over and I got a yes.

R: I think you're right. I think she doesn't want to leave the other ones who are also afraid. They all just need to go together as a group and be reunited with their families. There is no judgment, none of that over there. It's all love.

You'll find your family, your friends, people you've worked with. They're all over there.

DB: Let me ask the woman who's here, is this group ready and willing to cross over now.

A pretty hefty yes.

R: I think some of them are already gone.

DB: They may be … if somebody is holding them back they may just not want to leave them. Or her. I mean that's a guess.

R: Dwight, why don't you finish up?

D: Well, I'm too muddy.

DB: Yeah, Dwight's having an off day. I mean, I can feel it over here.

D: I'm just not clear. I was over by the tree, but I'm not here.

R: For me it was the exact opposite. I felt her. I saw her, but I think that's why she wanted us to come here.

So, everybody out! I want everybody to cross over.

DB: Some have already crossed over. You're right on that. I got a yes.

R: I want everybody to go. Go find that peace. Go find your families. Go listen to some Bowie. Oh, you don't know who he is—excellent music.

DB: They're not familiar with David Bowie.

There might have been a piano player someplace.

R: Go find the people you were familiar with. Find that peace. And if you want to come back to Gleeson or Tombstone you can do that. But follow the crowd.

You're welcome.

DB: I mentally asked if we've done all we can do and I got a little drop in the pendulum. That's a pretty good signal. When I said have we done all we can do here today I got a pretty good yes. See, I'm getting a real swing yes now.

D: Yeah, that's a big swing yes.

DB: I think we were drawn here to do what we just did.

R: I think there's a reason we met up with Bob and the stories we got from those people.

DB: I felt an attraction to this corner for some reason, also. I don't know why, but I felt it out there.

Is there anything more that we can or should do today while we're here?

No.

D: No, that's kinda' the feeling I'm getting.

DB: And she's the one who can go back and forth, so we're not talking to a trapped person here.

Would you like to say something into our recorders here?

R: These little boxes are … they'll record your voice.

DB: If you could at least say your name, please.

(Sound)

Stomach rumble.

R: It's a grasshopper.

D: It's really quiet for a Saturday.

DB: I think you nailed it with the little girl helping people cross.

R: Well, I think she—I don't want to say ministered to the people at the tree. I think she was their angel, so to speak.

DB: Yeah. Yeah.

R: The light of their day. She wasn't just bringing them their meals. She was a refreshing energy.

DB: Well, we did what we think we ought to do.

R: Yeah.

DB: I hope it's appreciated.

D: I don't think they get too many people who come here to actually talk to them. I think they just come here to—

R: Snap pictures.

D: Or demand from them.

DB: To confront.

D: To confront them more than to talk to them.

DB: I'm going to end my session here.

Closing session now.

It seems that maturity as measured on the other side is a matter of personal growth and development rather than in years. The angel who came back through the veil to help the souls trapped in Gleeson is a perfect example. A quote from Isaiah (King James Version) comes to mind. "The wolf also shall dwell with the lamb, and the leopard shall lie down with the kid; and the calf and the young lion and the fatling together; and a little child shall lead them."

The EVPs

D: What else was this building used for?

EVP: (coughing from two or more people)

For further reading on Gleeson ghost town:

gleesonarizona.com

www.legendsofamerica.com/az-ghosttowntrail.html

To listen to the EVPs go to:

www.beelieveparanormal.com/our-book.html

12

Knocked Out

When paranormal investigators are told in no uncertain terms to get out of a haunted area, that demand could be a threat, as in one of those "Get out!" scenes in a horror move. The message could just as well be a warning from a concerned spirit. That's the situation we faced when exploring an abandoned mine shaft near Tombstone.

We had heard about the place during a pleasant conversation with some of the locals living around Gleeson during the events covered in chapter 11. No one knew the history of the mine, just that it was large, very old, and might be of interest to a group of paranormal investigators. Much of Arizona, especially in the mineral-rich sections such as the Tombstone area, is littered with abandoned mines and mining prospects.

Dan and Dwight are walking down into the Perseverance Mine.

The names and histories of the miners are often lost to history. Bringing that lost history out of the darkness is one of the factors that motivate our efforts.

We went there on a lark. The site was nearby, easy to reach from the highway, and we figured we'd give it a try. The mine is accessed by bushwhacking through an overgrown gully. It was covered in brush and extremely hard to see until we were right on top of it—a long, dark shaft angling down into a rocky hillside.

We made our way in slowly and cautiously; this was during the summer and we were walking in prime diamondback rattlesnake country. Fortunately, we didn't run across any hostile or fearful critters. We did have a ghostly encounter that raised the hair on the back of our necks and put a fast end to our investigation.

We named the place the Perseverance Mine.

DB: Okay, this is our afternoon session. We are down, way down in a mine shaft. EVP session … go ahead, Dwight.

D: We're several, a few hundred feet down, give or take. We're at the point now where there is very little light from the entrance so we're going to stop here. If there's anybody down here with us other than us, come up and talk to us if you'd like. Come up to the little red light and talk to us and we'll be able to hear you on this.

(Noise)

D: And that was Rhonda.

R: Yeah. I was on a little uneven surface.

DB: I'm going to do a little pendulum work anyway, but go ahead.

R: Is there anybody down here with us? I already knew the answer. It was a yes.

DB: Yes, I got a yes.

R: Did you work here in the mine?

DB: One second. Got a yes.

Just for the record my back is to Rhonda. She can't see how the pendulum is swinging.

R: Did you die here in the mine?

DB: Got a yes.

R: For the recorder purposes if you could tell us what you were mining, that would be great. Was it silver?

DB: I got a yes on silver.

Mentally, I asked "gold" and got a no.

R: Okay. Was there a cave-in?

DB: Yes.

R: Yes.

Do you need any help from us? Are you okay? Okay, one question. Do you need any help?

DB: Null answer.

R: Dwight, what about you?

D: I'm getting a real strong answer. I don't mean to be rude, but I get the feeling that you want us to leave. Is that correct?

DB: I got a pretty good yes.

D: That's what I thought. I'm getting a lot of...

R: We're not after your silver.

D: No, we don't want your silver. We don't want anything to do with this place other than we knew it was here and we wanted to come down and visit it.

DB: I'm getting a "we are not welcome" here.

D: That's what I got, too.

So, okay.

DB: We just dropped in to say hello. That's all.

R: Yes. That's it.

D: The first rule of doing this stuff— we only do what the locals want us to do. If you want us to leave we will respect that and we will slowly, but we will be getting out of here. I want to thank—

DB: Whoa!

R: What?

DB: He wants us out now. Right now. I got a strong yes and then a pendulum jump.

R: Okay, we'll skedaddle.

D: We understand. We'll go on out now.

DB: That was a definite pendulum jump.

R: Thanks you for letting us in here.

DB: We appreciate it.

D: Yep.

DB: Would you say "goodbye" or "carry your ass" for us? Because we are leaving.

D: Yes, we are.

R: If you want to make something at the other end … kind of like an echo.

KNOCK

R: Oh, I just heard that. Did you?

DB: I did, too.

R: Did you hear that?

DB: Yes.

Can you do that again?

KNOCK KNOCK

DB: I heard it again. Was that in here or up there?

R: That was in here.

DB: Because I heard it twice.

R: So did I.

DB: Should we get the hell out of here?

D: That may be what they call tommyknockers.

R: Yeah.

D: It's what happens just before a cave-in.

R: Yeah.

DB: Well, let us remove ourselves.

But when you asked that … I forget what your phrasing was, but should we leave or are we welcome here I got strong reaction.

D: I was getting strong, like …

DB: And I got goosebumps on top of that.

R: "Get the F out?"

D: I mean, you know when you're facing somebody who's really angry and you can almost feel the heat coming off them. That's what I was feeling down there. I was feeling this heat on the side of my face like "get out … we want you to get out."

DB: Well, my pendulum responses were pretty strong. When we got to that subject. So we're leaving!

D: We're leaving.

Ending my session.

Unseen by Dwight and Rhonda, my pendulum indicated that we should leave the mine. This reaction came at the same time my two associates received the same message through their intuition. The knock we heard confirmed our reactions. Yes, we were in an old structure subject to falling debris and that knock could have certainly been a naturally occurring event. Notice, however, that the second set of knocks came immediately after we requested an auditory sign confirming the message for us to leave. The knock-knock came right upon the question "Can you do it again?"

Was that a rock falling at just the right moment or was it a spirit response? We believe it was the latter.

We skedaddled.

13

Working on the Railroad

A paranormal investigator doesn't have to enter the neighborhood haunted house at midnight on Halloween to encounter spirits of those who have passed on. Nighttime "ghost hunting" at "the witching hour" makes for good stories, but paranormal encounters can happen anytime and at any place. For example, most of the encounters related in this book occurred in broad daylight and many of them outdoors in open spaces. It makes sense. People pass away at all hours of the day and night. They all have memories of events that happened at all hours of the day and some of them have chosen to return to those happy times. Whenever we went on an investigation, we tried to remember that a good paranormal investigator is an alert investigator. We were always trying, and sometimes succeeding, in recognizing opportunities for contact whenever and wherever we were.

Sometimes an investigator can have an encounter seemingly by coincidence, an event so seemingly normal that the realization that a paranormal encounter has just occurred hits after the fact. Such is the case when Dwight and Rhonda were walking down the abandoned railroad bed towards the ghost town of Charleston, Arizona. The bed is built up above the flat lowland that is the ancient San Pedro River bed and provides an excellent view of the brush-and-weed covered surrounding landscape below. The bed is covered in a deep layer of metallic slag, rocks that crunch when stepped on. As they walked along they suddenly noticed a young black man approaching. He was dressed in a polo shirt, clean and pressed tan slacks, and walking shoes—not at all the appropriate dress for hiking that country. He walked confidently, as if with a purpose, and as he passed by he said, "Be sure to stay hydrated."

A few steps later Dwight and Rhonda had one of those "wait a minute!" moments. The young man had made no sound walking on the slag as he passed by—an impossibility. They turned, but he was gone. They had an unobstructed view of the railroad bed and the open country on each side, including the parking lot nearby. The young man had just disappeared.

Sometime later we were conducting research for the Charleston chapter in this book. We decided to explore this encounter. On the way back we did a short intuitive/pendulum session at the place where the young man had suddenly appeared. We recorded the session and picked up an EVP that said "Vamos," which means "let's go" in Spanish. We were worn out from our excursion and our sessions in Charleston, so the session was brief. We vowed to return.

Before returning Rhonda conducted an extensive search of possible identities of the young man. She even made contact with the family of the most likely person on our list. Not surprisingly, the family had mixed feelings about contact. The man's mother held deep convictions about the afterlife and was not open to contact or even hearing of contact. His sister was much more open and seemed interested in the information we were gathering.

Several candidates for the spirit fit the profile fairly well. One was named Raphael,* the most likely candidate, so we used that name as an identifier in our investigations. I conducted a map dowsing session to locate a possible site for locating human remains. Map dowsing involves a series of yes/no questions used in conjunction with a map to locate a specific area or place. In this case I used a topological map of southern Arizona and created a "shrinking box" by defining east/west and north/south points and gradually shrinking the four "edges" of that box to an area about the size of a football field. (When we returned this area had been washed out by the river.)

Just in case the individual we hoped to contact was someone other than who we believed, during my session I used the identifier "the person we are calling Raphael" rather than just "Raphael." That slight modification covered all our bases.

We came back to the railroad tracks February 5, 2017. We walked a short distance down the railroad bed to a point about the length of a football field from Charleston Road just north of the San Pedro River bridge. We started at a bluff that is 40–50 feet above the river. We conducted a pendulum session just to get our bearings on the case and the location. Dwight recorded the session, which produced a definite EVP. We asked a number of questions and discovered the fact that the male spirit we were addressing had chosen to return to the site so that he would be in a position to help people in distress or danger. One danger, dehydration, is a severe problem for people walking under the harsh Arizona sun.

DB: This is EVP session one for me. We're still at the bridge. February 5th. It is now 9:30 (a.m.). We just conducted a pendulum session and this is just a follow-up EVP session.

R: If anybody's here you can speak into these little boxes that the guys are holding. Speak into them really loud so we can hear you. Shout out your name or anything you want us to hear.

D: If the male who was with us during the pendulum session, if you're still here with us, you can shout out your name if you want to. That would be great so at least we can …

R: So we know.

D: … come back and talk to you specifically. If anybody else is here with us or the gentleman we talked to before, can you tell us if you can what you died from? How you died?

R: Did you drive up to this location?

DB: Were you dumped or dropped off at this location?

D: Let me ask this since it just kinda' came to me. Did you drown near here? Because that's what I'm picking up.

R: It could have been in the summer months, you know and …

D: If you drowned could you either say yes or no if you drowned.

R: Really loud because we've got background noises … cars.

D: So let me ask you one more time so we're clear, did you drown here or near here?

Okay, thank you if you answered us.

R: I have to ask. What do you think of President Trump?

D: We're getting a lot of traffic noise now. That should be pretty good.

DB: Let's see what we come up with.

R: Thank you.

DB: We do appreciate it.

I'm ending my session now.

We had an incredible experience walking east from the bluff toward the railroad bed for our next session. We were walking in line—Dwight, Rhonda, and me as "tail-end Charlie" when a clearly audible male voice speaking in conversational tones said "hello." We were in an open field and no one was within half a mile of us. The nearest people were three hunters down river at Charleston and two young men on the south side of the bridge. Remember, the riverbed was several stories down from our location. Again, the voice was clear and from someone right with us. His voice stopped us in our tracks.

DB: Let's do that again.

DB: I'm going to repeat myself. All three of us heard a voice. This is about five minutes to ten. We were walking back to the parking lot and the three of us heard a voice. It sounded like "Oh" or a lot like "hello." We all agree that it was a male voice and very near. So if that person is still with us we would like you to say something into this little box here, please.

R: And there's the hunters.

DB: Where are the hunters from here?

R: The sounds were coming from up that way.

DB: That wasn't the sound we heard at all.

R: No. That was the hunters we saw walking along the river.

DB: They're to the north of us. The voice we heard was to the west.

R: Southwest.

DB: Yeah. Towards the river.

R: Behind us. Behind us literally five or ten feet.

DB: It was not a shout.

R: No!

DB: It was a "hello."

R: Yeah.

DB: And we all agree that it was a male voice.

R: Yes.

DB: Well, give us a shout out, please.

Car door slam.

R: Car driving across the bridge.

DB: We've got to go now, so if you have something to say this is the time to say it.

R: Or come with us.

DB: Yeah, come with us.

R: You're more than welcome.

DB: But we appreciate the greeting anyway.

D: Yeah.

DB: End EVP session two for me.

We moved on and within a few minutes were standing on the railroad bed at the exact place where the original encounter had occurred.

DB: This is my EVP session number three. We're on the abandoned railroad tracks just north of the parking lot. February 5th about five after ten. We're just trying to contact the young man that Dwight and Rhonda saw, so if you're here, if you have anything you'd like to say, and if you have a sister, if you'd like to say anything to your sister.

(Gunshots from the hunters.)

But we understand that your sister would like to hear from you so if you've got anything to say we could certainly convey the message.

D: Just to make sure we're talking to who we want to talk to …

R: You should get out your pendulum after we do this so you can confirm.

D: We're looking for Raphael. And just to confirm, Raphael, for validation so we know it's you, can you tell us what your sister's name is?

KNOCK

R: That's me knocking on the recorder.

D: One more time, if you can tell us what your sister's name is. Come up real close to us and just …

R: Shout it in one of these boxes.

D: As loud as you can, that'd be great.

R: Well, these are little mini recorders.

D: Of course, the wind's starting to pick up now.

DB: I'm blocking the wind from my pendulum with my body.

R: Let me …

DB: Yes … I asked the person "that we are calling Raphael" here and I'm getting a yes. Somebody heard.

R: Let me find out something here.

DB: Another yes.

D: A lot of traffic noise out here today.

R: Okay, there we go. So, Raphael, are you here?

DB: I'm getting a firm yes. Somebody's here.

R: Is your sister's name Sofia**?

DB: I'm getting a yes.

R: And are you fifteen?

DB: I'm getting a null, so … Were you fifteen when …

R: Were you fifteen when you died in the car accident?

DB: That's a yes.

R: If you have any message for Sofia or your mother we can help you do that.

DB: That would be a yes.

R: I have a feeling that you stay with your mom quite a bit.

DB: Again, that's a yes.

R: Unfortunately, because she's so devout in her religion …

DB: Swinging yes.

R: … she doesn't feel you, feel your presence, or hear you. We're hoping that your sister can help her, her grieving process, help her understand that you're still around.

Are you the young man that Dwight and I saw on the railroad tracks?

DB: That's a pretty good yes.

R: Do you stay out here and help people. Or do you come out here and help people.

DB: That's a good swing yes.

R: Let me ask this, do you help other spirits?

A little bit?

DB: A weak yes.

R: Do you mostly try to help the living, to make sure they're always doing the right thing?

DB: That's a strong yes. He was just taking care of you guys.

R: We appreciate it.

Sofia told me that you liked to come out here and hang out with your friends, hang out with your buddies.

DB: That's a yes.

R: I can certainly understand why. This is one of our favorite places, as well.

You guys want to ask any specific questions?

D: No. I'm just letting the recorder run.

DB: This is your chance to say something.

D: At this point he knows what we're doing out here so if he wants to talk …

R: The good thing is we've got a bunch of your friends that know now that you're out here trying to help people. I posted a message on Facebook and so many of your friends were in awe that you're still hanging around and they miss you dearly. So what was your favorite sport? Apparently he was an athlete.

DB: That would explain the walking.

(Dwight and Rhonda said that the young man walked with a purpose. He wasn't ambling.)

R: This could be where he trained or whatever.

Do you have any messages for any of your friends who were in the car with you that day? If you do, just speak into the recorder.

DB: Before you ring off, this is what it sounds like when you walk on this gravel.

(**DB** footsteps on a slag railroad bed.)

DBL: Dwight and Rhonda say when he came by this is what they heard:

(**DB** stops walking.)

R: There were our two sets of steps, but once he passed us we didn't hear the crunching of the rocks, which is when we turned around and there was nobody there.

DB: It's impossible to walk on this track without making noise, because we've tried.

R: Yeah, you can't recreate somebody walking up and then not hearing them. And even if they did you'd see them out in this scrub brush out here. Because it's not very thick or very high.

DB: Ending my session now.

*Not his real name. Out of respect for the beliefs of a family member, we are using a different name.

** Not her real name.

The EVPs

R: Yes.

DB: Would it be fair to describe you as something of a guardian-type angel?

EVP: Yes

R: We appreciate you talking to us.

DB: It's impossible to walk on this track without making noise, because we've tried.

R: Yeah, you can't recreate somebody walking up and then not hearing them. And even if they did you'd see them out in this scrub brush out here. Because it's not very thick or very high.

EVP: What gives?

DB: That would be a yes.

R: I have a feeling that you stay with your mom quite a bit.

DB: Again, that's a yes.

EVP: Hey, you three.

R: Unfortunately…

To listen to the EVPs go to:

www.beelieveparanormal.com/our-book.html

14

Checking Out of the Gadsden Hotel

Douglas, Arizona, was established on the Arizona-Mexico border, founded in 1901 primarily to house smelters for the copper ore that was dug out of the ground in nearby Bisbee. The town also served the interests of miners, cattlemen, ranchers, and businessmen in the area. One of the finest hotels in the Southwest was built downtown. The five-story Gadsden Hotel, named for the famous Gadsden Purchase, opened in 1907.

Tourists still drop in to marvel at and photograph the luxurious two-story lobby, which features a grand staircase of white Italian marble.

Dwight and Rhonda in the lobby of the Gadsden Hotel.

*Dan is using a pendulum to communicate
with spirits in the Gadsden Hotel.*

Legend said that the chips missing from some of the steps were made by the hooves of Pancho Villa's horse as the bandit hero rode up the staircase. Four massive marble columns in the center of the lobby are accentuated by 14k gold leaf ornamentation. An authentic Tiffany stained glass mural running 42 feet across the mezzanine wall is one of the few Western scenes ever created by Tiffany & Co. Stained glass skylights run the length of the lobby. It is a stunning sight.

A fire occurred on Feb. 7, 1929, and destroyed everything except the marble staircase. The Gadsden was rebuilt on an even grander scale. The new hotel featured an electric elevator and something novel for that time—individual bathrooms in all 160 air-cooled rooms. At one time there was even a speakeasy housed in the basement.

Throughout the twentieth century, the Gadsden was a happening place. Hollywood discovered the opulent location and many movies, TV shows, and videos were filmed in the hotel.

Dwight and Rhonda had encountered a gentleman spirit during an earlier visit and we were hoping he would drop in to say hello to the three of us. We began down in the basement, which had served as the speakeasy many decades earlier.

This session illustrates why we're so careful about double-checking EVPs, sounds, and events. Commonplace actions or events can easily be mistaken for paranormal occurrences. For example, as you will read below the sounds of automobiles crossing a metal grate can travel through a building to sound like human voices. Lights and shadows can play tricks on the mind. Someone speaking on a cell phone a hundred yards away can sound like genuine spirit communication. When recording we always called out extraneous sounds as they occurred so that we didn't have to rely on memory when listening at a later time.

Our recordings are full of:

"Bee."

"Traffic noise."

"Water bottle."

"Helicopter in the distance."

"That was me."

It was amazing how easily it was to mistake a normal sound for a captured EVP. Our careful approach allowed us full confidence in reporting our encounters.

Note again, we were always committed to capturing good-quality EVPs, but we never considered them as artifacts to be collected and stored like rare coins or stamps. They make one of many forms of validation of our work. The EVPs were never the primary goal. We found them to be helpful research tools in learning the history of a site and its people, and in learning the needs of spirits requiring our help.

DB: This is EVP session one, Gadsden Hotel with Dwight and Rhonda. Setting my recorder down on the pool table.

R: I just turned off my camera, so ... all this shut off here ...

D: Okay, we'll just leave the recorders out.

R: Hey, Mister, if you're here come over to the pool table and talk into this little box with the red light. I know you're here.

DB: We're in the speakeasy ...

D: Yep.

DB: ... beneath the Gadsden Hotel in the basement.

R: Tell us what your favorite drink was.

DB: I'm getting that he likes straight whiskey. If that's true would you confirm it with maybe a yes.

D: Whiskey or scotch?

DB: I'm getting scotch.

R: With the pendulum.

DB: I asked for Kentucky bourbon and got a no. I asked scotch and got a yes.

R: Big yes.

DB: A man after my own heart.

R: (Laughs)

DB: Or liver as the case may be.

D: Yeah, exactly. Exactly.

Well, we're going to be walking around here today upstairs, downstairs, everywhere so feel free to join us and come along with us.

R: Dan, can you ask with your pendulum if he just really … if he sees the speakeasy as it was when he was alive?

DB: Do you see the speakeasy as it was at the time when you were alive? (positive swing)

R: Yep.

DB: Can you see it as it is now? Weak yes.

R: Yes. So it is your choice to see it as you prefer it?

DB: Strong yes.

Are you here by choice? Do you want to be here?

A very good yes.

R: Keep your pendulum out because I want to take a picture as well.

DB: You're here because you want to be here.

(Beep.)

R: My camera.

DB: That's a very strong yes.

R: Are you wearing a tux, sir? A very fancy jacket?

DB: That's a yes.

D: That's the same guy as last time.

R: Yeah, I'm pretty sure.

Is your name William?

DB: I'm getting a no.

R: Does it begin with a W?

DB: I was asking something else.

R: Okay. Sorry.

DB: Go ahead. Go ahead.

R: Does your name start with a W?

DB: I'm getting a yes on that.

R: Is it Bill? So is it William, but you go by Bill?

DB: Don't mean to interrupt, but I was asking 'Was it Bill' at the same time. We got the same thing.

R: He didn't like William. Maybe that's it. He didn't like the name.

DB: Yeah.

R: Okay. Bill, thank you very much.

DB: We overlapped each other there.

R: Intuitively that's what came to me.

DB: I was asking "Bill" …

R: Same time as I was thinking it as well.

DB: That's scary.

R: Hey, Bill, do you ever see the little boy that's down here as well, the little boy that passed.

DB: Yes.

R: Do you know if he's okay? Is he with his family?

DB: No.

R: Does he need help crossing over?

DB: Yes. Big yes.

R: Okay. Thank you, Bill.

DB: Strong yes. Wow.

D: We encountered him over by the lift.

R: Yep.

Thank you so much, sir, for your time.

DB: Do you know the guy in the maintenance room? Yes.

R: Is he okay here? Is he here by choice?

(DB positive swing.)

R: That's what I thought.

DB: Let me do that one again. Ask it again.

R: Is the maintenance man here by choice on this ... okay?

DB: Double confirm. My hand just jerked a little bit and I wanted to double check.

Is the maintenance guy a friendly guy?

(Negative pendulum swing.)

D: No.

R: Nope.

D: Nooooo ... (laughs)

R: Seriously, last time we were here he led us to believe he liked being back there working on stuff away from everybody else. Is that correct? He does not want any people contact?

DB: Yes.

R: He's a loner.

DB: Yes.

R: He has to work. You know, he has to make a living, but he does not like people.

D: I'll record this for posterity ... there it is. Got it. (Takes photo.)

DB: Snap one of me with my camera.

R: He did.

D: Oh, I did two while you were doing your session. It's almost like I'm an intuitive.

DB: I see Fred Peeples. (Movie reference joke.)

D: Okay. Let's move on. I'll stop the session.

R: Okay.

DB: Okay, Bill, thank you.

R: Be seeing you, Bill.

D: Ending EVP session one.

DB: Ending session one.

We were guided on our tour by one of the Gadsden Hotel employees, Adam. He was with us all the time although not always near us. This led to some confusion over a photographic image, which we were later able to debunk.

DB: EVP session two. We're down in the lift section of the Gadsden Hotel trying to speak to a little boy who passed here.

D: If you would say hello that would be great.

R: Yeah. Yell really loud and we can record it and we can record your voice like a picture on this little box. You need to go find your mom and dad. They're over there waiting for you. I know there are lots of people over here for you to play with, but you need to really go through the light and find your parents, honey.

(Background noise.)

D: That's street noise for recording purposes.

R: Was that a car?

D: Yeah, it's the street right here so you can hear the car. There's a grate up there they go over so it sounds like voices.

R: Yeah. I think it is the man in the top hat. He followed us here to see what we're doing.

D: Well, he followed us last time.

R: Yeah. To make sure maybe that we're helping? You want to talk to the little boy, babe?

D: I have been.

R: Okay. You can come back. You just need to go check in with your parents, honey. I promise.

What was that shadow?

DB: Down there.

R: Okay. It freaked me out for a second. It felt like it was right behind me. It went across. Was that Adam? Okay.

(Shout in distance—Adam.)

DB: … all the way down there.

R: Would the shadow come up this far because literally …

DB: What would make the shadow? Because that light is too high.

R: Somebody walked to this. I was looking... Turn around and look.

DB: Yeah.

R: See.

DB: There's a shadow here. He is making a shadow.

D: Yeah, but he's not making it on the back of the wall here.

R: Yeah. He's right there.

DB: It's coming up to me.

R: Okay, but the shadow is on the back wall.

DB: Well, no. He wouldn't make that.

R: That's where I saw it. That's what freaked me out. Adam's shadow only comes halfway up into this doorway.

DB: It comes up to where I am, but it's not on the wall.

R: That was...

DB: I'm going to set my recorder down.

Just step out...

R: Are you going to get a picture?

(Voices in background—Adam on phone.)

Okay, so Adam's talking in the background.

D: Yep. There was a shadow that just went across so it is ... Oh, he's got a flashlight.

Yeah, so there is some movement there.

R: But I don't think he was right there with a flashlight when I saw the shadow.

D: Probably not.

(Noise in distance.)

R: That's interesting.

DB: I'd have to bet that's Adam down there, but I didn't see him when I took the picture.

D: Well, when you send me I can put it on the computer and blow it way up and then I can see ...

DB: If he's got a phone in his hand it'll definitely be Adam.

D: Or a very hip ghost.

DB: Or a time traveler.

D: Yeah. Time traveler.

DB: But I swear I was looking over the camera and I did not see anyone when I took the picture.

D: We can certainly ...

R: I took a picture of us in the dark because I can ...

D: Okay, so we're going to head out now. You can follow us if you want. We're going to be here for a little bit.

R: (Whispering) And go find your dad and your mom. Find 'em.

D: That was Rhonda whispering.

R: Sorry.

D: There we go. And end EVP session two by the lift.

DB: Ending session two.

I took a picture showing a human figure down the hallway near Adam's position. Later research proved that the image was Adam and not a materialized spirit. The shadow we saw was something entirely different and is still unexplained.

We believe we helped the boy check out of the Gadsden and to cross over to join his family. The well-dressed gentleman who enjoys a good shot or two of scotch seemed quite happy where he is and in the time frames in which he exists. We saw no need and felt no inclination to urge him to leave a place where he seemed so happy to stay. We moved on and he stayed as a guest in the heyday of the magnificent Gadsden Hotel.

The EVPs

DB: I believe it's an artifact. I'll look on my screen when I get it.

R: We need to help this little boy cross over, so…

EVP: He didn't do it.

To listen to the EVPs go to:

www.beelieveparanormal.com/our-book.html

15

Breakout at Hoptown

As the shadows cast by sunrise faded from Tombstone, the darkness lingered longest in the Chinese quarter. Of the town's population of approximately 5,000 people, 300–500 were Chinese. They were, for the most part, a hard-working group of people who kept to themselves and maintained their cultural traditions. Like many towns in the Old West, Tombstone suffered from the malady of racism. The Chinese were welcome to work, but they weren't generally welcome in the parts of town occupied by whites. They traveled through town underground in a series of tunnels. Because they hopped in and out of those tunnels, their community became known as Hoptown.

A panoramic view of the Hoptown area of Tombstone,
Arizona, circa 1940. Courtesy Library of Congress.

The community was connected to the rest of Tombstone, but was at the same time mostly a self-contained unit. The small community included groceries, gambling halls, restaurants, laundries, and even a temple that was used for worship and as a meeting place.

Many in the community were known by their nicknames. For example, a Chinese male might be known as John and a female as Mary. These names often appear in the official US Census.

Hoptown's most prominent resident was one of those named Mary. Nee Sing, sometimes called Ah Chum, was known as Chinese Mary and she was the "queen bee" of Hoptown. She was a plump woman who favored brocaded silks and jade jewelry in the Chinese fashion. She bridged the gap between two communities, providing reliable laborers for the families and businesses on the white side of town. Her motto was "Them steal, me pay."

If the work performed wasn't up to the employer's standards, China Mary redid it for free. She also ran a general store stocked with goods for each community. She ran a gambling hall in the back of the store, one of the few places where whites and Chinese mixed openly. The character of China Mary even made it into a 1960 episode of *The Life and Legend of Wyatt Earp*. She was portrayed by actress Anna May Wong.

Wyatt's Hotel and Coffee House and the Saloon Theater now sit on a site once occupied by a general store operating during China Mary's heyday. Town records show that 225 Allen Street was the site of a store owned by Quong on Chong, who featured Chinese goods. We couldn't find a record of any murders or killings at that location. Considering how most people felt about the status of the Celestials, events in Hoptown probably weren't "above the fold" reading in the local newspapers, assuming they even made the newspapers at all. It's impossible to know what unrecorded events occurred in the back rooms of many local establishments in all quarters of Tombstone. The Chinese, like the rest of the people in town, were a tough bunch. They had to be.

The theater is historic in the sense of what happened here in the past, but the building is new. Reenactors dressed in period costumes recreate famous Arizona gunfights on a regular schedule, making the facility a prime tourist attraction.

As we discovered in an emotionally charged moment, the theater was also an attraction for those old enough to remember China Mary, Wyatt, Doc, Curly Bill, Ringo, and the good times and bad times in Hoptown. One poor soul, in fact, refused to leave and preferred to be a spirit trapped in Hoptown rather than move on to a better life on the other side.

In an unplanned session watched by dozens of people and recorded in audio and video, we helped this spirit end his time in a self-imposed prison. Virtually everyone in attendance was emotionally affected. As the expression goes, by the end of the session "there wasn't a dry eye in the house."

A Haunting in the Desert

Dwight and Rhonda's *A Haunting in the Desert* is a three-day event that includes presentations and demonstrations by premier psychics and paranormal investigators, tours of historic sites in the Tombstone area, and direct participation in paranormal investigations of haunted sites.

As with any series of events dealing with those who have crossed over, the results of contact vary considerably. Sometimes very little or nothing at all occurs. Other times genuine contact is made. Sounds and voices can sometimes be heard clearly and even recorded as EVPs. And sometimes, *sometimes*, the experience can become so emotionally powerful that it is overwhelming. That is precisely what happened during *A Haunting in the Desert II* at the Saloon Theater in Tombstone's Hoptown.

Saturday (May, 21, 2016) had been a full day—a long day, but an exciting one. Dwight, Rhonda, I, and guest presenter Brian Cano of television's *Haunted Collector* led two groups through the abandoned mining community of

Gleeson. Later the group was given a tour of Tombstone's St. Paul's Episcopal Church, which was established in 1882. Dwight and Rhonda had also arranged for a tour of a unique feature of this boomtown's first church—a brothel, which had been located just behind the church on church property. There is a reason it was called the Wild West. The last event of the day was a paranormal investigation of the Saloon Theater in which the attendees could participate.

Dwight and Rhonda were the organizers and managers of the event. I considered myself "grunt labor" and helped whenever and wherever I could. We were tired and had planned on taking it easy during the event. Brian was the scheduled director of the evening's activities, so management and labor had few responsibilities that night. The front half of the theater was set up with rows of chairs. The back end featured a simulated 1880s bar. About half of the group took to the chairs with the other half "bellying up to the bar" to conduct the research.

As planned, the evening was to be a low-key event. The attendees would spend some time directly with Brian. They would hang out with a television personality and at the same time directly experience a simulated paranormal investigation. I found a place to sit down at the far corner in the front of the building, leaned back, lowered my hat and pretended to listen with my eyes closed. Rhonda took a seat on a staircase about halfway down the room. Dwight stood at the rear of the building. All three looked forward to an easy evening of observing Brian and the others try to make contact.

Dwight said, "The expectations were really low as to whether we were going to connect with any spirits and that kind of thing. The energy was palpable even then, but I think that was more from the attendees than it was anything else."

The documentation of paranormal activity in the building was sparse. There were reports of a photo that showed a ghostly apparition on the stairs midway through the building. Still, the site (if not the building) was located in an historic part of a well-haunted city and the investigation was worth the effort. Even if no one from the other side made an appearance the experience of conducting an actual investigation would be rewarding for the attendees. Again, Dwight, Rhonda, and I stepped back, anticipating minimal participation. This was Brian's show.

Rhonda was confident of the possibility of a successful investigation. The moment she stepped into the theater she psychically saw two men standing on the stairs—two spirits. She sat down not too far from them. To her, they seemed to be observing the event with some interest.

When a site has been occupied by more than one building throughout the years the spirits often inhabit the site as it was when they passed. Sometimes they are able to observe and interact in the current facility. In our work we have encountered some who expressed surprise or confusion at the new faces and unfamiliar scene of the current property.

The attendees began by using triggers to stimulate paranormal activity. Triggers are physical objects familiar to those who have crossed over that might enhance contact. For example, in the simulated bar at the theater, liquor bottles, shot glasses, beer mugs, cards, and poker chips were used. They were recreating a typical night at a Tombstone saloon, hoping the familiarity would bring about a response.

Early on they received a couple of legitimate EVPs of two spirits—one of them a murder victim. They were encouraged and continued in their efforts to make more contact.

I had given my pendulum dowsing lecture earlier so one of the participants was encouraged to try that technique. She was new to dowsing and was using a pendulum she had purchased that day. This was her first effort and she was making a valiant effort for a first-timer. In addition to her lack of practical experience she was working in a strange environment and surrounded by people she didn't know. On top of that the evening was being documented by a production crew out of New York. That was a lot of pressure. She struggled and was doing as well as could be expected.

Brian asked Dwight to come up to the bar to help out with the session. He worked with the young woman with the new pendulum. After a few moments Brian looked my way and asked if I had brought my pendulum. "No."

Dwight said of what happened next, "We were on the wavelength of just staying as far out of it as we could, but one-by-one Brian asked me and he asked you (Dan) to come over. It was interesting to me that you didn't even have your pendulum. You kinda' improvised, adapted, and overcame. There was a girl right next to you who had a long silver necklace with a cross on. You asked to borrow it and said, 'Okay, we have a pendulum. Let's do this.' That's when you and I started working the questions. You and I have worked together before so we knew each other's energy and were working the questions and 'bringing in the box' a little bit further." Bringing in the box referred to the technique of asking questions in which each one narrows the field of focus until the answers become more and more specific and related to the given situation.

It's important to note how I held the pendulum that night. There are two basic techniques. One is to hold the chain or string between the thumb and forefinger. The other is to wrap the chain once or twice around the index finger. I was using the second technique.

Dwight and I discovered that two spirits were present. One had been murdered and one was the murderer who apparently died in or near the location at a later date. Rhonda said, "I think the people were under the impression that they were talking to the victim. But they were actually talking to the person who did the killing."

She also said that the spirits were present and not just residual energy. They were curious about the simulated activity at the simulated bar. In their time the place had been a general store and they wondered about all the fake gambling and drinking going on.

Paranormal research is serious business, but that doesn't mean the researchers lack a sense of humor or are afraid of expressing that humor even in public, and in this case, on camera. Dwight took charge of the session and began asking questions. I used the improvised pendulum as a means to get the answers.

Dwight said, "Is there someone here who can help you?"

"I'm getting a yes," I said.

"Is this person a male?"

"No."

"Is this person a female?"

" … well … *duh*, Dwight!"

The room burst out with laughter.

"I don't think Brian or the production crew was expecting that," Rhonda said.

A moment and a few barbs later it was back to business. The tension had been broken, but the energy was rapidly ramping back up. Dwight honed in on finding the person who could help the spirit of this murderer, although each man knew what the answer had to be.

"Does this person's name begin with the letter R?"

"Yes."

We continued to shrink the box to make sure the person with the R name really was Rhonda, Dwight asked the spirit if he was trapped.

I was immediately hit and overcome with a wave of profound sadness. It was sudden, without warning, and overpowering. Someone in the group snapped a photograph at that very moment. It's somewhat of an embarrassing photograph because my mouth was wide open as if I was clowning around. In fact, the photo shows my initial reaction and my desperate efforts to control my emotions.

"We need Rhonda up here," I said.

So much for coasting through the evening.

I motioned her to the bar and she came up immediately. She later said other than the initial impression of two spirits she felt upon entering the theater, she had received no further psychic messages until the paranormal research intensified. As she approached the bar those powerful emotions washed over her.

I could see the change as it happened. The closer to the bar she got the more emotional she got. By the time she made it to the bar she was crying and could barely speak. She said, "It was as if I were there and I knew these two persons and they were my relatives. It was grief. That's the way to explain it."

Instead of sitting back and zoning out of the session, Dwight, Rhonda, and I were now center stage of a dramatic and emotional drama. Brian was right in the middle of it, but the spirits had reversed the roles. He was now more of an observer experiencing something quite unexpected. As Rhonda arrived, Dwight felt the energy immediately ramp up. From that moment on, the movements of the pendulum were stronger and more pronounced. The energy could be felt, and by that time most if not all of the attendees were feeling it.

Rhonda said, "I was in a zone. I don't remember anybody. I don't remember questions. I don't remember seeing anybody. All I remember is seeing the tunnel and seeing these two men. And I knew there was a helper there. It was like both of them were trapped and, like we've experienced before, like a caseworker, a helper, or whatever you want to call it. Somebody to help them move on. But more so the murderer. That's what I thought."

The three who had planned on "sitting this one out" continued asking questions and seeking to discover the needs of the spirit and to see if there was a way to help fill that need. At some point Rhonda took control of the session, although at the time she didn't realize it. The team was so focused on their efforts that the attendees, the production crew, and even Brian faded into the background. The psychics were unaware of anyone else in the room and were absorbed in what we were experiencing.

The questions became affirmations. Rhonda discovered that the spirit of the killer was afraid to cross over—fearing judgment and eternal suffering.

She said, "You don't have to be afraid. You can go. You have permission now. You can go. It is safe." This comforting and reassuring process continued for a couple of minutes.

Many of the attendees were also affected by the emotion in the room and were sniffling and crying. Some were scratching their heads. No one was unaffected.

Dwight described what happened next. "And the pendulum pretty much snapped tight." There was an audible sound and that's what got Brian's attention. He even mentioned to us later that it was an actual sound and an actual tactile feeling. He said he even felt it. Brian has had experiences in possessions and that kind of thing. He likened it to when a priest does an exorcism and the priest is successful: it doesn't happen over a graduated amount of time; it happens right now. He said it was the same type of situation. "When they leave they leave immediately. (Snaps fingers.) It wasn't like they're going … they're going … they're going … they're gone. It was like 'boom' and that's when you said, 'They're gone.' And just before you said that the pendulum dropped. The wrap that was over your finger actually came over your finger to drop."

After the release there was a collective "ahhhhh … " from the attendees. Some of them wanted to continue the questioning, to get more answers, but that was impossible. The paranormal investigation part of the evening was over. The trapped spirit had been freed and had moved on. Twenty-four attendees, Dwight, Rhonda, Brian, and I felt something powerful. Many of the attendees were crying and others were fighting back tears. They had experienced something truly rare and wonderful. Emotionally, it was draining.

Brian had an interesting take on what had happened. He said, "This time because Dan was there and you guys were there and I figured *okay I've done my EVP session*, we got an interesting EVP about a murder. Someone asked the question, 'Did you murder anyone? Did you kill anyone?' And the response was immediate: 'Yes I killed someone.' And everybody heard it—in front of the recorder as well as across the room...

"I figured this would be interesting since we were on Dan's turf and Dwight and Rhonda's turf, let's get them to do the next round. I wanted to see the pendulum in action. And from there, having you guys focus and 'construct the box' to get more specific with the information. By the time you guys called Rhonda in we had identified that there were a couple of spirits. One of them had been murdered. He was unsure what to do. He didn't know if he could move on or what would happen.

"A bunch of the other attendees started to get very emotional. When Rhonda was pulled in I knew she was emotional too. And I was thinking, 'Wow! Something is going on.'

"Then by the time it all came to a head and the energy dissipated and you (Rhonda) said, 'It's okay. You have to cross over. You've gotta' move. And the pendulum ... I don't know if I was imagining it, but there was a snap, a tiny sound, and the pendulum jerked and stopped. And Dan just put his head down and said, 'He's gone.'

"At that point I wasn't really sure how to react. What to do. In Hollywood this type of occurrence would be accompanied by shafts of light and harp music and a chorus. But here this was amazing and quiet and I've seen exorcism videos of the same thing and they're very jarring given how little is going on.

"I remember afterwards, not that I was skeptical, but I wanted to follow. You guys are used to this. You do this all the time, so I needed more info. And my main thought was, 'How do we know we're doing good? How do we know we're doing the right thing?' But I was super, super gratified to be a part of this and the mean take away of this, beyond just do good work, was look at the overlapping of disciplines here. We had technology, an EVP that got the response for us to pull in the dowser to say, 'Okay, let's get some more information,' followed by the energy work … it was teamwork in different disciplines. And it was great because all of the attendees saw that you don't have to choose one or the other. It's all part of the teamwork."

Someone might ask, "How do you know what happened was real?" Believe what you want, but we were in a legitimate 'lights-camera-action' scenario, but I'm just not that good an actor. The emotion I felt, and what the others felt, was overwhelming. We didn't manufacture that emotion. It was brought to us by the spirits we helped.

It's food for thought, but perhaps one of the reasons Tombstone is "the town too tough to die" is because so many of the dead and gone haven't really gone. Others in Tombstone and other locations will surely find a release as we continue to convince them that it's okay to at last cross over—that their time served is over.

The EVPs

"Yeah, I killed somebody."

(EVP courtesy of Brian Cano)

To listen to the EVPs go to:

www.beelieveparanormal.com/our-book.html

Conclusion

We began our paranormal research as an experiment. It has become something of a quest. Dwight, Rhonda, and I are among those fortunate few who are able to do what we love pretty much whenever we want. We combine our love of history and our deep interest in the paranormal with the opportunity to help people who, though passed on, are continually experiencing the worst moments of their existence. The soul-satisfying and incredibly emotional feelings we get from helping those people is indescribable. We sincerely hope we have been able to share some of what we do and what we love.

We've only been at this unique place for a very short period of time as things are measured, and we have far more questions now than when we began. I assure you that we will continue to seek the answers.

Stay tuned.

Marcus F. Griffin

Foreword by Jeff Belanger

EXTREME
PARANORMAL

INVESTIGATIONS

The Blood Farm Horror,
the Legend of Primrose Road,
and Other Disturbing Hauntings

Extreme Paranormal Investigations
The Blood Farm Horror, the Legend of Primrose Road, and Other Disturbing Hauntings
MARCUS F. GRIFFIN

Okie Pinokie and the Demon Pillar Pigs. The Ghost Children of Munchkinland Cemetery. The Legend of Primrose Road. Join Marcus F. Griffin, founder of Witches in Search of the Paranormal (WISP), as he and his team explore the Midwest's most haunted properties. These true case files of extreme paranormal investigations include the creepiest-of-the-creepy cases WISP has tackled over the years, many of them in locations that have never before been investigated.

Readers will get an inside glimpse of these previously inaccessible places-such as the former Jeffrey Dahmer property, as WISP searches for the notorious serial killer's spirit—and the farm that belonged to Belle Gunness, America's first female serial killer and the perpetrator of the Blood Farm Horror.

978-0-7387-2697-7, 264 pp., 5³⁄₁₆ x 8   **$15.95**

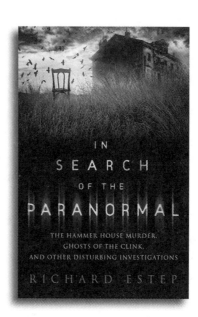

IN
SEARCH
OF THE
PARANORMAL

THE HAMMER HOUSE MURDER,
GHOSTS OF THE CLINK,
AND OTHER DISTURBING INVESTIGATIONS

RICHARD ESTEP

In Search of the Paranormal

The Hammer House Murder, Ghosts of the Clink, and Other Disturbing Investigations

RICHARD ESTEP

From exploring the Tower of London to investigating a haunted Colorado firehouse, paranormal researcher Richard Estep takes you behind the scenes for an up-close-and-personal encounter with a fascinating legion of hauntings. This collection reveals some of the most chilling, captivating, and weird cases that Richard has investigated over the past twenty years, in England and in the United States.

In Search of the Paranormal is filled with rich historical detail, present-day research, and compelling eyewitness accounts. You are there with the team at each haunted location: walking through a desecrated graveyard, shivering in a dark basement, getting thrown into the Clink, watching a "ghost-lit" stage in an old theater. Employing a variety of investigative methods—from high-tech gadgets to old-fashioned practices such as dowsing, table tipping, and Ouija boards—Richard Estep and his team uncover the dark mysteries of the paranormal realm.

978-0-7387-4488-9, 264 pp., 5¼ x 8   **$15.99**

To order, call 1-877-NEW-WRLD
Prices subject to change without notice
Order at Llewellyn.com 24 hours a day, 7 days a week!

The House Where Evil Lurks
A Paranormal Investigator's Most Frightening Encounter
BRANDON CALLAHAN

This is not a Hollywood tale; it is a true account of the most malevolent home that Brandon Callahan and his team have ever investigated. A former funeral parlor, the demon-infested property had a dungeon and a sinister past that included murder, suicide, and vile rituals.

When Brandon Callahan answered the homeowner's plea for help, he had no idea what he was getting himself into. A monstrously tall entity in a dark-hooded cloak moves through the embattled home it considers his domain. An expressionless phantom follows one of the investigators home. Innocent bystanders and paranormal investigators alike are plagued by physical attacks and bleed-through phenomena: inhuman laughter, bloody scratches, disembodied shrieks and growls, horrific nightmares, and escalating threats. *The House Where Evil Lurks* is Brandon Callahan's terrifying true story.

978-0-7387-4066-9, 264 pp., 5³⁄₁₆ x 8   **$15.99**

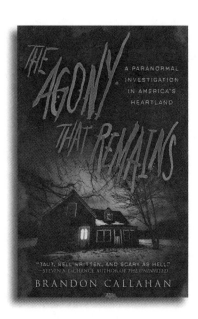

THE AGONY THAT REMAINS

A PARANORMAL
INVESTIGATION
IN AMERICA'S
HEARTLAND

"TAUT, WELL WRITTEN, AND SCARY AS HELL."
—STEVEN A. LaCHANCE, AUTHOR OF *THE UNINVITED*

BRANDON CALLAHAN

The Agony That Remains
A Paranormal Investigation in America's Heartland
Brandon Callahan

In the northeast corner of Oklahoma, where the deadly path known as the Trail of Tears ended and where one of the world's large clusters of ley lines intersect, there's a place of extreme paranormal activity that has received little attention from the outside world. Join Brandon Callahan and his crew as they investigate the horrifying legacy of a bloody and brutal past, where generations of families have been terrorized by ghosts, demons, UFOs, little people, Bigfoot, and countless other paranormal manifestations.

Teaming up with a family who has been driven from their land, Brandon and his crew discover energies that have no fear. As dark forces begin taking hold of the investigators' lives, Brandon must attempt to salvage what's left of his team's—and his own—sanity.

978-0-7387-4793-4, 360 pp., 5¼ x 8   **$16.99**

To order, call 1-877-NEW-WRLD
Prices subject to change without notice
Order at Llewellyn.com 24 hours a day, 7 days a week!

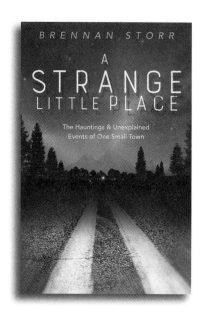

BRENNAN STORR

A
STRANGE
LITTLE PLACE

The Hauntings & Unexplained
Events of One Small Town

A Strange Little Place
The Hauntings & Unexplained Events of One Small Town
BRENNAN STORR

Embark on a fascinating journey into Revelstoke, Canada, a world-renowned ski destination with a well-kept secret: it has a long and active paranormal history just as breathtaking as its mountain views. Packed with stories of hauntings, UFOs, Sasquatch, missing time, and much more, *A Strange Little Place* takes you into a small town full of thrilling secrets and bizarre encounters.

Chronicling over seventy years of unusual occurrences in his hometown, Brennan Storr provides exciting, first-hand accounts of unexplainable phenomena. Discover the sinister mysteries of Rogers Pass, the strange craft and spectral music of the Arrow Lakes, and generations of hauntings in the infamous Holten House. As a magnet for the supernatural, Revelstoke invites you to experience things you never thought possible.

978-0-7387-4823-8, 264 pp., 5¼ x 8   **$15.99**
